# SIX LITTLES GO A LONG WAY

# SIX LITTLES
# GO
# A LONG WAY

~

James Little

First published by Arena Books in 2025
www.arenabooks.co.uk

*Six Littles Go A Long Way*

ISBN Paperback: 978-1-914390-43-2
ISBN Ebook: 978-1-914390-44-9

A catalogue record for this book is available from the British Library

Thema: WTM; WTL; WTHW; WTHY; DNC; DND; 3MPQV; 1MBF; 1FKA; 1FCA; 1FBN; 1DTT; 1D; 1DDU

BISAC: BIO026000; TRV010000; TRV000000; HIS037000; TRV003000; TRV004000; TRV009000;

Cover design by Arena Books
Book design by Arena Books

Printed in Great Britain

*For Mum*

# CONTENTS

# Foreword

As I sit in my Singapore hotel room in April 2024 awaiting a replacement flight to the UK after our A380 was turned around due to technical problems, I am reflecting on what this book is really about. The experience of being forced into a common plight with 500 other travellers over two days has been enlightening. Everywhere I look people are talking to each other and smiling. It's as if we have been given permission to communicate and like withered plants just watered, we are coming back to life. What would normally be the object of our primary interaction – our smart phone – is now other people. Talk of frustration with BA – with some passengers claiming it typifies broader decline in the UK – quickly gives way to more personal discussions about the reason for travel, where people have been and where they are going. Everyone is interested, interesting and enjoying the nourishment that conversation with strangers provides, and which smart phones and AI can never hope to deliver. That, I feel is what this book is about.

*Julian (32), Peter (3), Mark (6), James (7), Andy (6 months), and Becky (29)*

# Introduction

My mother and father met in London in the mid-1960's whilst undertaking their medical training – Dad as a doctor, Mum a nurse – at Charing Cross Hospital. One of their common passions was travel, especially to far flung places. As Dad recalls, talk of an overland trip had cropped up early in their relationship, although at that time it was only a pipe dream.

Mum – Rebecca (Becky) Evens – grew up in working class Crayford, daughter of Charles, a drafstman engineer, and Mavorneen, a nurse. Becky was not a fan of school and was desperate to spread her wings, jumping at the chance, at 18, to train as a nurse in London. Dad – Julian – grew up in Surrey, the son of a chest physician, George, and Ninette, who moved with her sister from South Africa in 1937 and made England her home. Perhaps this is where some of Dad's wanderlust originated from, but I think with both of my parents that it was more to do with the combination of their personalities and the freedom and excitement of the post war era. This was London in the swinging 60's – the age of the Beatles, hippies, free love and discovery.

My parents married in 1969, and I was born in June 1970. Just six months later they were off on their first adventure, driving a Morris Minor all the way down to Split in current day Croatia, then Yugoslavia. It was a sign of things to come.

Dad retells the story of the events which led up to their move to Australia in 1974:

"It was Mike and Fran Carrette who persuaded us to go to Australia. Mike had been a year above me in Medical School, qualified and then started training in Obstetrics/Gynaecology. Fran was in the same set as Becky and I had known her from before, as she was the daughter of a doctor who had worked with Grumpy [Dad's father, George] at Hydestyle Hospital near Milford, Surrey. Anyway, Mike and Fran got married and disappeared off to Cairns.

"Early in 1974 they came back to England so Mike could do his final specialist exam in O and G. They asked Beck and I around for dinner and showed us these very alluring and beautiful photos of Cairns and surrounding beaches. Half-jokingly we said that if ever an Anaesthetic post cropped up in Cairns, we would be interested.

*Farewell gathering at 71 Park Road, Chiswick, 1974*

About two months later, when we were living at 71 Park Rd, Chiswick with Rob and Kate, we received a telephone call in the early hours of the morning. A vacant Anaesthetic post in Cairns had suddenly cropped up, but we had to decide within the next five days. No problem in making that decision, but I had to give notice. However, within the month we were on a plane out to Australia, I to take up the post of Junior Consultant in Anaesthetics, even though I was not yet fully qualified. That is how we ended up in Cairns, Beck and I and our two boys."

We loved living in Australia – the wide-open spaces, the freedom, friendliness of the people and the outdoor living. My brother Mark, who was born in London in 1972, and I don't have many memories of Cairns, but For Mum and Dad, these were memorable days, with leisure time centred on the outdoors; swimming, sailing, camping, scuba diving and more. The beaches of North Queensland are some of the best in the World and with the Great Barrier Reef so close, this is a fantastic location to sail and scuba dive. It was in Queensland that my parents bought the Toyota HiAce camper van which was to become our home for 6 months.

As Dad remembers:

"Becky and I continued to keep the idea of an overland trip in the back of our minds whilst in Cairns, but it really wasn't going to be feasible or practical due to the huge cost that was involved. When Peter was born, [1975], we thought if we were still to do it, we might as well carry on with three Children; after all we were prepared to do it with two. The same reasoning when Andy was born in Adelaide [1977]. Rather naive of us I suppose, but we were young and yearned for adventure.

The big thing that changed when we were in Adelaide and made us think it might be possible after all, was a change in our financial situation. I had started some private practice on the side which was quite lucrative and adding substantially to our income. One other thing that persuaded us we should return to England was Mavis, your grandmother, [Mum's mum – another force of nature]. She was in and out of hospital for her drinking problem. At that time, she wasn't acutely ill, [she would become so], but we thought we should return before she deteriorated too much. And so, the decision was made!"

I recall that Dad was a 'Flying Doctor' as part of his Cairns General Hospital role, as part of a GP Service or 'Flying Surgery' for remote communities. He was one of the anaesthetists, part of a whole group – surgeon, anaesthetist, nurses, technicians – who would fly by helicopter into the Outback, where they would carry out simple operations like sterilisations, circumcisions, growth excisions etc. More serious cases were referred for hospital treatment and because of the distance involved patients would often have to be evacuated by air. The private practice Dad was involved in in Adelaide was always carried out in a hospital or private clinic and had to be conducted outside normal working hours, so most often in the evenings.

Having lived in Cairns and Adelaide for a total of 4 ½ years, Becky and Julian were keen to see more of Australia before we returned to England. On Monday 31st October 1977 – Halloween – the six of us left Adelaide in our Toyota camper on the first leg of a 15,000-mile, 6-month road journey back to England. Whatever madness made my parents attempt this journey with so many little Littles, packed into a camper van, I will always be truly grateful for. There were some hair-raising moments, but the people we met and experiences we had in those six months, were formative for me. Forty-five years later, on Halloween 2022, I started typing up my parents' diaries, also a Monday, with a view to writing this book. My weekly Sunday Facebook blog of our previous seven days' travels 45 years on, elicited many welcome contributions from family and friends. The research and writing experience revived many memories for me, not only of the trip but also of dear old family friends and, most of all, my mother and force of nature, Becky, who died far too young.

*Becky (29), Mark (6), Andy (6 months), Julian (32), Peter (3), James (7)*

# PART I
# AUSTRALIA
## *(2,284 miles)*

~

*Australia: Our route crossed the Nullarbor Desert, only recently tarmacked and home to the longest straight section of railway in the world.*

Map © 2025 Google

# Chapter One

# Anama Farm

*Monday 31st – Sunday 6th January 1978*

In reviewing our route, I wondered why, as were headed to Southeast Asia, we didn't take the northern highway through Alice Springs to Darwin. This would have put us much closer to our next destinations, Bali and then Singapore. Dad explains, "Roads inland were dusty tracks; no tarmac, and mud bound in the rainy season in the East. We would have needed a four-wheel drive, and it would have been dangerous; not wise with four young children." This sets the benchmark then of what Becky and Julian Little regarded as too dangerous, though as our story unfolds, it becomes clear that not much else was off the table ...

Instead, Becky and Julian decided to head over 2,000 miles west on the Eyre Highway across the Nullarbor Plain – tarmacked only the previous year; luxury by comparison to most inland roads of Australia in the late 70's. Firstly though, we had some Merino sheep farming friends to visit in Burra and, in the chaos and haste of leaving Adelaide on Halloween 1977, plenty more preparations to make.

### Day 1 (Monday 31st October 1977) – Leaving Adelaide

**Becky:** *Today was exhausting. We hastily left Jane and John's, who were getting a bit sick of us in the end. Everything became jumbled in the camper van. Trying to do the shopping with a camper van fully loaded for our Asian trip plus four children was a bit of a joke. Nevertheless, we almost succeeded in getting* *everything, though arrived at the pharmacy 10 minutes after it closed.*

*Tried to phone Penny three times from Adelaide. The phones are as difficult as can be if you haven't the right change, then the phone is broken. Anyway, didn't leave town until 6pm. Having revisited 101 Watson Ave – finding a super parcel with a dress for me and photographs from Martin and Hilary – we then visited Pizza Palace then set off. I had persuaded Jules to stay in a motel for the night, but we couldn't find one after getting out of town, so we ended up camping beside the road, Jules and I squashed in the roof. Andrew and I in one sleeping bag after his vaccinations. In spite of the hard bed, we slept well.*

**Julian:** *Eventually left John and Jane's about 11am. Glad to be away because of the obvious strained feeling which had cropped up between us. Perhaps we had overstayed our welcome. As a result of our haste to be away though, the van was in absolute chaos and obviously overloaded. We were also feeling exhausted from the strain and numerous social commitments of the last few weeks. To make things worse it decided to drizzle constantly throughout the day. I almost drowned riding my putt-putt to Grace Brothers for transportation to Anama [Penny and Jamie's farm]. As we rushed around town with four kids in the rain, I wondered whether this was a taste of what was to come.*

*Refreshed ourselves at the pizza place and feeling slightly improved left Adelaide for hopefully the last time. The luxury motel we intended to treat ourselves to never turned up and we still found ourselves on the road and too late to phone Penny up. We 'camped' by the roadside and squashed in amongst the rubbish totally exhausted.*

We had to quit our Adelaide home – 101 Watson Avenue – before we were quite ready to hit the road. Mum and Dad's friends, Jane and John kindly put us up for a few nights. However, it sounds as though we overstayed our welcome. Dad remembers, "We weren't very organised people like they were, who always had everything in it's right place"; I think his use of their best dinner forks to repair a puncture on one of our bikes wasn't the most sensible idea.

We were on our way to the farm of good friends Penny and Jamie Hawker near Booborowie, 100 miles north of Adelaide. Arriving the next day, we stayed for a week, drawing breath, and preparing for the start of the journey proper across the Nullarbor Plain. Re-reading Mum's first diary entry, it struck Dad 'There were no mobile phones in those days; how times have changed!' Regarding the 'putt-putt' he also recalls:

"We only had the Toyota van then, and so that Becky wasn't trapped at home, I bought this little scooter to get to the three hospitals [three!] I was working in then. I left it with Penny; heaven knows what happened to it."

*Adelaide Halloween Farewells*

### Day Two (Tuesday 1st November) – First morning on the road

**Becky:** *Well at least we slept in spite of Andy waking almost immediately after we fell asleep. I thought we were in for a night of it, as he would not be comforted by a feed – I think it must have been a cholera jab reaction. It was a hard sleep, as Julian and I were in the push up roof with no mattress, but we were too tired to care. In the morning it took about two hours to unpack and repack. When we drove off, I looked back and remarked at the spaciousness of the camper. Julian did too, and suddenly realising why, we burst out laughing – we had driven off with the camper roof up, luckily not too fast otherwise the* *strong wind would have ripped it off!*

*We arrived at Penny's half an hour later. No one rushed out to meet us and we wondered why until we met Penny at the door and found that her horse had died at 2am during a difficult birth. She was very upset, but our arrival started to take her mind off it. We lazed around most of the day, all feeling a little bit the worse for wear from the strain of the last two weeks. Went to bed at 8:30pm feeling exhausted and relieved to finally be able to relax.*

### Day Three (Wednesday 2nd November) – Jingle Bells and sunsets

**Becky:** *A really good night's sleep in spite of various interruptions from Andrew and Peter. Penny went to playgroup taking James, Mark with Rosemary. Somehow, I didn't get much done – Peter was difficult, so was Andrew, (as much as he ever is these days), and Alice cried to go out. However eventually when lunch was over and I had succeeded in tipping coffee over, leaping to stop Alice tipping up her pot – two catastrophes! – I started sorting. Not much success at getting rid of things so far. Managed to do the washing. The kids had a lovely ride on the horse Jingle Bells – they thought it was 'great'! Had another pleasant evening meal with Penny (James at expensive sheep sale). Eventually went to bed at 11pm. The most beautiful sunsets here.*

### Day Four (Thursday 3rd November) – Wakefulness

**Becky:** *The kids waking up even more. Marky wet, so feeling slightly the worse for wear this morning. We went to town in afternoon, rushed around like lunatics trying to get all the shopping, but there seems to be plenty more to do. Kids got tired and hot and we didn't return until 6:15. Another wakeful night including thunder; the baby woke every two hours and was a bit colicky during the day, perhaps a reaction to the cholera jab. Peter absolutely grotty!*

### Day Five (Friday 4th November) – Stay and rest a while

**Julian:** *Another hectic day at Penny's with me preparing the van and Becky sorting out clothes. Had intended to leave Saturday morning but were persuaded to stay for the weekend in order to relax. Penny and Jamie went to dinner with*

*Sarah and Andrew and stayed overnight. Rosemary was left with us.*

## Days 6-7 (Saturday 4th – Sunday 5th November) – Sorting, packing and playing

**Julian:** *Supposed to have been relaxing weekend but we continued to sort and pack. Persuaded to stop one more day to take things easy. Kids seemed to have a good time. James and Mark helped Big Jamie, and Penny took all the kids for a ride on Jingle Bells.*

*Kids' Playtime*

Chapter Two

# The Nullarbor

*Monday 7th – Sunday 14th November*

The Nullarbor Plain is a flat, almost treeless, arid part of southern Australia, located on the Great Australian Bight coast with the Great Victoria Desert to its north. It is the world's largest exposed limestone bedrock and features the longest stretch of straight railway (297 miles) in the world. English explorer Edward John Eyre became the first European to successfully cross the Nullarbor in 1841 and the highway is named after him. In writing of Eyre's voyages in 1865, Henry Kingsley described Nullarbor as a 'hideous anomaly, a blot on the face of Nature, the sort of place one gets into in bad dreams.'[1] This was the longest section of our journey in Australia and from the journal entries, (or lack of them), it sounds as though it was truly exhausting. My memory of this section is hazy, but the diary tells the story…

**Day 8 (Monday 7th November) – Nearly ready**

**Julian:** *More fiddling around with van and sorting clothes. Penny and Becky made the 'clothes hanger' while I tried to keep the kids from interrupting. Quite a warm day requiring a few splashes in the pool. Further rides on poor Jingle Bells for the kids.*

---

1  E. Littell, E, *The Living Age*, Volume 87. Boston: Littell, Son and Company, 1865. p. 481.

**Day 9 (Tuesday 8th November) – Away at last**

**Julian:** *Spent all morning packing van with children clambering in and out. Stayed for lunch with Sally Hawker and a visiting South African lady. After numerous piccies and goodbyes we eventually set off at approximately 2.45pm. Day beginning to warm up. Port Augusta and Whyalla are real dumps and very hot. Pizzas at Whyalla. Evening continued to heat up (35°C). Hot air blasted in through the windows. Eventually reached Arno. Had beer in pub and stealthily pitched camp in caravan park next to the sea exhausted.*

*Leaving Penny and Jamie's*

Australia's seasons are at opposite times to those in the northern hemisphere, so things were just beginning to warm up to summer as we began our journey across the Nullarbor. The only caravan park next to the sea in Arno, a small fishing and tourist town on the east coast of Eyre Peninsula, is Arno Bay Caravan Park. Dad agrees that is probably where we stayed – from the 300+ pictures in the Google Maps entry it looks pretty spectacular, dominated by a mixture of white, sandy beaches, cliffs, and mangrove systems. Particularly impressive is 'Redbanks', a sedimentary cliff structure which is a designated geological monument by the Geological Society of Australia.

For the next two days there are no diary entries, but Dad recalls we followed the coast road through Port Lincoln and camped in Coffin Bay; named in 1802 by British naval explorer Matthew Flinders in honour of his friend Sir Isaac Coffin, Resident Naval Commissioner at Sheerness, where his ship the Investigator was fitted out.

We had reached Streaky Bay by Thursday 10th November, where the scenery again is impressive. The name Streaky Bay was given by explorer Matthew Flinders, who says in his log of 1802: 'And the water was much discoloured in Streaks ... and I called it Streaky Bay.'[2] It is now thought these streaks are caused by the release of oils by certain species of seaweed in the bay.

## Day 12 (Friday 11th November) – Ceduna

**Julian:** *A hectic morning of breaking camp with kids screaming and arguing. Pleasant couple next door gave us some hints about crossing the Nullarbor. Eventually left about 12 noon and after shopping left Streaky Bay about 1pm. Beautiful sand dunes and beaches along the stretch of the bay proper. Stopped at Perlubie beach before Ceduna. Cup of tea and drinks at garage in Ceduna. 100 miles out of Ceduna, 'tea' in parking lot.*

The name Ceduna is a corruption of the local Aboriginal Wirangu word Chedoona and, appropriately, is said to mean a place to sit down and rest. The 'parking lot' 100 miles out of Ceduna appears to have been a petrol station, Mobil Nundroo, described in Google Maps as a 'Casual 1950's hotel with restaurant/ bar'. Dad thinks it was here that we camped on the night of Friday 11th. Some of the buildings certainly look as though they were there in 1977.

---

2  Matthew Flinders, *Log*, 5 February 1802. 'Streaky Bay - Our History.' *Wayback Machine*, Internet Archive. https://web.archive.org/web/20070829215502/http://www. streakybay.sa.gov.au/site/page.cfm?u=194

The lack of a diary entry again for Saturday 12th November hints at endless hours of monotonous driving. Dad mentions in his entry of Sunday 13th that we camped in a parking lot, which must have been across the State Border between South and Western Australia. It took us an hour to get to Balladonia, which would have put us somewhere around Caiguna. The signpost pictured below with directions and distances to big cities of the world, (just 17,517 km to London!), was at the imaginatively named 'Border Village'.

*Below: Old road grader memorial to the building of the Eyre Highway*

The Eyre Highway, (named after English explorer Edward John Eyre), which crosses the Nullarbor had only recently been tarmacked and just a few miles later at Eucla we stopped to clamber onto a discarded grader which had been used and left as a memorial. I found some fascinating YouTube footage on the building of the highway and the opening ceremony unveiling the memorial, which was held at Eucla on 29th September 1976, just over a year before our crossing.[3] Unfortunately, the grader became so corroded that by 2003 it was scrapped.

### Day 14 (Sunday 13th November) – Time travellers

**Julian:** *Because of the time change, (1¾ hours back at state border), we were away at an incredible time for us. We had camped in a parking lot and with Beck feeling really efficient, we had packed up in a matter of an hour in the midst of a dust storm. Feeling filthy and with everything covered in dust we set off on another day of drudgery and monotonous scenery. Straight road, scrub bush and nothingness. Another ¾ hour back at Balladonia one hour later gave us an extra advantage. Fish and chips at Norseman for lunch and the end of the Eyre highway. A turn south and off to Esperance, the scenery improving somewhat and becoming greener, arriving there approx. 16.30. Taking four hours to set up camp, feed and bed the children we collapsed, feeling rather depressed and wondering whether it was all worthwhile.*

On reading this I was struck by how exhausting it must have been for Mum and Dad driving across the desert with us four young kids; we had covered 778 miles in two days. And yet, we were still only just at the start of what would become a 15,000-mile journey back to London. What an undertaking, especially with Mum just 29 and Dad 32 years old. Many times, my parents have been told they must have been crazy! Growing up with the memories and stories, I started to take the experience for granted, but in re-living our travels through the diaries and in creating this book – slightly mad though they were – I can honestly say I am really proud of them for doing it.

Another revelation of the diary entries to me, was that time zones in Australia can change by two and a half and even one-and-three-quarter hours! Some states have daylight saving and others don't, but as we were driving west, clocks every so often would go back and we would gain time. That was why we were able to cover the vast distance to Esperance in just

---

3 '1976 Eyre Highway sealing ceremony,' *watvhistory*, YouTube, Feb 1 2012, https://www.youtube.com/watch?v=pafZk2bTyY4.

two days. At that time of year, the majority of Western Australia was two and a half hours behind South Australia, but Eucla and Balladonia has its own time zone, three quarters of an hour ahead of the rest of Western Australia. So, in a very short space of time, we crossed two time zones gaining two and a half hours.

Before Standard time was introduced in the 1890s each local city or town was free to determine its own local mean time; Eucla's GMT+ 8:45 persevered, making it part of the smallest time zone in Australia, Australian Central Western Standard Time (ACWST), comprising just a few hundred people. One theory is that this came about because the operators of a telegraph station based in Eucla in the 1800's found it more convenient to be closer to Australian Eastern Standard Time. Whilst not recognised as an official time zone to this day by the State or Australian Government, keeping ACWST suited the local inhabitants who ran the roadhouses on the Eyre Highway, as it meant they all shared the same time. There is something uniquely Australian about this 'just do it' attitude; so too when the State of Southern Australia unilaterally decided to advance Australian Central Standard Time by thirty minutes in 1899. Apparently, this followed lobbying by businesses wanting to be closer to Melbourne time, and cricketers and footballers who wanted more daylight to practice in the evenings!

Chapter Three

# Esperance to Denmark

*Monday 14th – Sunday 20th November*

The Aboriginal name for the town of Esperance is kepa (water) kurl (boomerang); it means, 'where the water lies like a boomerang.' Its European name was given by French explorers who named the place after their ship whilst sheltering from a storm in 1792. The name means 'hope'. After our mind-numbing crossing of the Nullarbor, the two days we spent here certainly appear to have given Mum and Dad renewed hope for the rest of our trip.

A little-known fact about Esperance occurred less than two years after we came through, bringing with it global attention. In 1979, debris from the Skylab space station fell onto Esperance after disintegrating over the Indian Ocean. In response, the local government issued a $400 fine to the USA for littering. This fine remained unpaid until April 2009 when radio host Scott Barley of Highway Radio raised the money through contributions from his morning show audience and settled the fine on NASA's behalf. The re-entry of Skylab was a global media spectacle, sparking the creation of souvenirs, bets on the exact time and location of its crash, and extensive news coverage. The San Francisco Examiner even offered a $10,000 reward for the first fragment of Skylab to be delivered to their office. Seizing the opportunity, 17-year-old Stan Thornton gathered fragments from his home's rooftop in Esperance, boarded the first available flight to San Francisco, and successfully claimed the prize. That's initiative!

### Day 15 (Monday 14th November) – Twilight Cove

**Julian**: *Unintentionally arose at some unearthly, uncivilised time because of the time change. Stood us in good stead though, as after a full morning of catching up on ourselves we still had a good part of the day left. Sausage sandwiches for lunch and then left for town. While clothes were washing at a launderette at a BP garage went to visit the Pink Lake. Really is very pink and exceedingly salty.*

*Surrounded by white sand dunes. On the way back, trunk blew off roof rack scattering all our dehydrated food over the road. Luckily only the trunk was damaged (cheap). Bit of shopping in town and then off to Twilight Cove. Beautiful coastal scenery, surf pounding in on wide open beaches and rolling sand dunes. Great games of hide and seek in sand dunes but too cold to swim. Back to camp for a 'quick' goulash in the pressure cooker. 3 hours later and with all the kids asleep we had worked out how it worked. Never mind the goulash wasn't bad!*

*Mum and all 4 boys*

*Dad with Andy*

**Day 16 (Tuesday 15th November) – Exploring and relaxing**

**Becky:** *Had another lovely day. Still seem to be 2 hours in front of everyone else. Went down along the 11-mile coast road to observation point; very beautiful. Ended up at Twilight Beach. Kids played with canoe and Dad while I sat on the beach. We even put the annexe up – the kids didn't remember seeing it before. Kept the car a bit cooler. Flies were awful. Managed to cook supper a bit better than last night's effort with the pressure cooker – Ha, Ha! Then went off to do the family's washing – haven't worked out how to do it with no effort yet* [though she does later – look out for the solution]. *Bed at 9.30. Lovely two relaxing days (apart from 5 to 7pm!).*

*Observatory Point, Esperance*

*Campter van from Observatory Point*

Twighlight Cove was named after a ship which was swept ashore during a storm on 24 May 1877. The area is susceptible to 'king waves' and several ships have been wrecked on its shores. The camper van annexe was a rarely used small tent attached to the back of the van for privacy whilst using the 'Porta Potti'. We lugged this portable chemical toilet all the way back from Australia to England (15,000 miles!) without using it once. It can be seen in the pictures on the van roof rack, still in its cardboard box, getting increasingly dishevelled as we clocked up the miles. I'm sure it seemed a great idea at the time... As well as the annexe, we also had a main tent which attached to the side door of the van and was put up almost every time we camped, often by 7-year-old me. (I must have had help but in my mind's eye I was a lone ranger!) This was Mum, Dad and Andy's sleeping quarters, while Mark, Pete and I slept in the pop-up roof of the van, which we loved – it was our own little den. The main camper space was used for cooking, eating and living.

### Day 17 (Wednesday 16th November) – Aboriginal Art and Albany

**Becky:** *$4.35 per night, camping site Esperance (62,900). 10.30 by the time we left. Went to a marvellous Aborigine Art place; left at 12.30. Got paper weight and shell broach for George and Ninette* [Dad's parents]. *Petrol at Ravensthorpe – 45 litres (63,035) – $7.30. What a dump. Carried on through Stirling Ranges. Looked lovely but too far to see properly. We arrived at Albany about 8pm. Too dark to see caravan site clearly, but Middleton Beach looked a dump, so we plumped for Emu Point Park. Full of trees, very nice. Chose our own site near the beach, though not quite on it. Can hear the waves at night crashing on the beach.*

Why the sudden need for noting prices and mileage I can only guess at – perhaps Becky and Julian had had a conversation about the trip budget. The Stirling Ranges, named in 1835 after the then Governor of Western Australia, James Stirling, has been a National Park since 1913. Being the only mountain range in the region, it attracts significant rainfall and is consequently one of the richest areas in the world for flora with over 1500 plant species; including more species of wildflowers, 'than in the entire British Isles,' according to the Australian Department of Climate Change, Energy, Environment and Water!

### Day 18 (Thursday 17th November) – Mount Clarence

**Becky:** *Messed about all morning. Andrew being difficult about sleep at present – hasn't adjusted to the new time and wakes up it seems all night. Weather overcast and gloomy. We both feel tired and a bit flat. Hung about the campsite too long sorting out. Got out at 2pm eventually. Went up Mount Clarence – spectacular view. Whole avenue of trees planted in soldiers' names up to the monument (First World War).*

*Went shopping – funny little town. Few really old buildings – church built 1846. Rather lovely food shopping. A bit of a shock – a few veggies nearly $12. I think I was done! Went around to Frenchman Bay and decided to return the next day. It was lovely. Got to bed really early and thankfully Andrew gave us a few hours before his nightly call.*

### Day 19 (Friday 18th November) – The Amity & a whaling station

**Julian:** *A lovely day. Beck feeling really efficient after her first three teas in bed. Got away by 09.30. Visited Amity Crafts in town and bought a super floppy leather hat for Beck. A quick whiz around the museum where we learnt all about the settlement of Albany. Kids loved replica of 'The Amity'. Then away onto the peninsular. Visited the Gap and Natural Bridge and whaling station. Was fascinating, only land based one in Australia, but the stench was overpowering. Peter was a bit horrified.*

'The Amity' was a 148-ton brig which brought the first settlers to several colonies in Australia, including Albany in 1826. Built in 1816 in New Brunswick on Canada's East Coast she was used to trade between America and Britain before transporting the Ralston family from Scotland to Tasmania in April 1824. She carried the first 70 European settlers, comprising 29 convicts, explorers and their families to Queensland in September 1824. Many places, including the town of Amity, are named after her. She was eventually wrecked while transporting cattle to Tasmania after running aground on an uncharted sandbar now called Vansittart Shoals on 18th June 1845. She was deemed to be a vessel of such importance that a full-sized replica was built in time for Albany's 150th birthday on Boxing Day 1976, meaning that she was less than a year old when we visited. Nearly half a century on and she is still enthralling young children with her stories of convicts, first settlers and castaways.

Peter wasn't the only one horrified by the whaling station but for my brother Mark and I, at 6 and 7-years-old, it also held a morbid fascination. Most of all though, I remember the stench and very nearly being sick. The station was operated by 'Cheynes Beach Whaling' from 1952 until 21st November 1978, the last land based whaling operation in the Southern Hemisphere. In that time the company caught and processed 1,136 Humpbacks & 14,695 Sperm whales, closing just a year after we visited. Whale oil was the finest oil known to man and was used in products such as Swiss watches and by NASA (in what I am unsure). The site re-opened in 1982 as a visitor attraction, 'Whaleworld' (now 'Albany's Historic Whaling Station') and attracts approximately 70,000 visitors per year.

*Natural Bridge on Albany Peninsula*

*Albany Whaling Station*

We moved on to Frenchman Bay, so named by the surveyor and Naval Commander W.E. Archdeacon in acknowledgment of the visits of French explorers Nicolas Baudin (1803) and Dumont d'Urville (1826) who replenished their ships from the fresh water springs that still flow into what is today known as 'Whalers Beach'. Dad remembers the sand was so fine that it actually squeaked as you walked over it – attributed to the fact that it is almost pure quartz with grains which are very fine and evenly ground.

**Julian:** *Sun was shining and not too hot and we had a good walk along the beach at Frenchman Bay, beachcombing and collecting some beautiful shells. Then up to Stony Hill Lookout where we got a superb view of Albany and Princess Royal Harbour. Newells Harbour came next and then the Blow Holes, which we didn't actually see, but we had tea there anyway. Back to Albany with a trip round Clarence Mount looking at old residences. Ended day with good old habit of fish and chips.*

*Beachcoming at Frenchman Bay*

**Day 20 (Saturday 19th November) – Sightseeing, Denmark and Jaffas**

**Julian:** *Packed up and left Emu Point campsite. First stop Emu Point itself for a swim, followed by pies (lunch 12.30pm). James previously very upset because of losing his 'Mother of Pearl'. Then visited a craft cottage, where we bought a money purse to hang around Beck's neck, followed by the Old Gaol Museum. Fascinating place – lady in bonnet to greet you, dark hole for naughty prisoners and a 'Hesian Refrigerator'. Strawberry Hill Farm was next on the list, built for Sir Richard Spencer, Government Resident of Albany in 1831. Devonshire tea afterwards and made the visit a real little piece of England. Another view from top of Mount but kids getting a little grotty by now and then off to Denmark. Not a long drive and countryside becoming lusher and greener with taller trees. Camped at Rivermouth as darkness was falling. Beautiful campsite surrounded by tall, green trees. No beach though. Jaffas and baked potatoes for supper.*

*Strawberry Hill Farm*

*Mark and I, Rivermouth Campsite with 'Jaffa Iron' in foreground*

I vaguely remember the trauma of losing my 'Mother of Pearl' shell – I thought it was so precious! Strawberry Hill Farm was the first farm in Western Australia, established in 1827 as a government farm when the first Europeans settled at King George Sound. Sir Richard Spencer, Government Resident, acquired the farm in 1833 and lived there with his wife, Ann, and his ten children. He added a granite two-storey building whose first visitors included Charles Darwin and Captain Robert FitzRoy, of HMS Beagle. 'Jaffas' are toasted sandwiches – Mark and I thought they were a real treat.

**Day 21 (Sunday 20th November) – Sailing & Dianne!**

**Julian:** *Did very little. Stayed at campsite most of the day sorting and mending. Local Rivermouth Sailing Club was having a race with catamarans. Made me very jealous. Beautiful day and not too hot. Walk in late afternoon to Denmark itself. Quiet place with not much going on. Usual game of Bowls with white hats and kids jumping into the river. Beck defied the law by picking wildflowers on the way back. Barbeque chicken for tea but we were rather distracted for who should walk out of the bushes waving merrily but Dianne! What a coincidence! On her way with a girl called Jan to Wyndhorn. They had only left Kalgoolie the day before, so we could have met her there. After much discussion she is seriously* *thinking of coming with us.*

As his comment suggests, Dad loves sailing. He built his own sailing dinghy – an Enterprise – as a school carpentry project when he was 13. His Uncle Ian Donald, (the inventor of ultrasound – honestly, look him up!), and Cousin Caroline first got him into sailing dinghies on family holidays in Holy Island, Anglesey and on the shores of Loch Fyne in Scotland. His first dinghy experience was in Holy Island at ten years old and was not auspicious. Caroline was teaching him the basics; he was already in the boat, and she was hanging on when a puff of offshore wind suddenly tore it, and him, from her grasp. Fast disappearing out to sea and not knowing what to do, with Ian shouting from the beach to pull in this or that rope and to move the tiller this way or that, he did eventually manage with some luck, to get back to one of the headlands bordering the bay. Strangely this experience did not put him off but made him more determined than ever to master the art; perhaps a bit like mastering the art of driving from Australia to England!

Master the art he did and inspired by Uncle Ian, who had built his two dinghies from kits, when he started at secondary school at thirteen, Dad decided to build his own Enterprise. To me this sounds incredibly ambitious, but with all the facilities of the carpentry shop at school, (helped by the fact it was Charterhouse!), and with the help and support of his carpentry Master, Dad built the boat in six months. Of course, these were the days when dinghies were still made of good old mahogany wood, not moulded plastic as nowadays. *Vol au Vent* ('Flying in the wind') as she was called – and now simply *Becky* after our mother who died in 2001 – is now in Bantry Bay, Ireland, with my brother Pete.

Another worthy tale of Julian's sailing exploits occurred several years later on a family holiday in Loch Fyne when he was sailing his own *Vol au Vent* on Loch Fyne with his cousins. The wind was light, the sun shining, and they were drifting along towing lines in the hope of catching some fish. Suddenly and without warning there was a massive disturbance of water off their starboard bow and a huge black monster slowly started to emerge from the depths – a Loch Fyne Monster? They immediately headed for shore, but not fast enough in the light wind, as the monster fully surfaced, and they realised to huge relief that it was a submarine!

In 1974 when we moved to Cairns from London, Dad bought a Sharpie sailing dinghy with a good friend, Peter. Although the Sharpie is/ was a thoroughbred racing dinghy with a genoa and trapeze, Dad used it mainly for pleasure and didn't do much in the way of racing. We just enjoyed pottering along the beautiful beaches with an occasional foray out to a tropical Cay, once even to tropical Green Island, part of the Barrier Reef and about fifteen miles off the coast. No wonder then on Sunday 20th November 1977 as Dad stood contemplating the Catamarans racing at Rivermouth, Denmark and the journey ahead, he sounds wistful!

The diary mentions Dianne emerging from the bushes as my parents are barbequing chicken. Dianne is a great Canadian friend of Mum and Dad with whom we are still in touch. They first met at Cairns Base Hospital where Dianne was one of a trio of nurses who were very close friends and did everything together. Dianne trained with my mother at Charing Cross Hospital in London. Betsy from Canada is Justin Trudeau's aunt, the recent Canadian Prime Minister of 10 years. Betsy's sister Margaret married Justin's father Pierre, (15th prime minister of Canada from 1968 to 1979 and 1980 to 1984), in 1971. Mum and Dad introduced Betsy to the man she married – Robin Dening from Cullompton, Devon – who was a Little family friend. Robin was a geologist who spent weeks at a time isolated whilst prospecting for gold in the Cape York Peninsula, often cut off by floods. When he did return to Cairns, he was desperate for female company, so Mum and Dad introduced him to their nursing friends, 'The Trio'.

Dianne did in fact join us for about half of our trip and we shared many wonderful experiences together. It is so strange to think that it was tonight 45 years ago as I write that we just happened to bump into her at Rivermouth Campsite, Denmark. Dianne now lives in Toronto and to my joy, we finally connected yesterday. She becomes a valuable contributor to our story, sending me her diary entries and giving another female perspective. She tells me, "I often talk about my time travelling with the Littles and the exploits along the way. When I do look back, I think how tolerant that you and Mark were as you spent so many hours just driving and without much 'free play time'." Thinking back, I don't remember ever getting bored, (though Dad may have a different story). We had our Lego and books and were experiencing so many new, wonderful, and sometimes frightening things. There simply wasn't time to get bored!

# Chapter Four

# Denmark to Yallingup

*Monday 21st – Sunday 27th November*

Bidding a temporary farewell to Dianne, we continued west via: the Valley of the Giants, where we parked our camper van inside a giant Red Tingle tree; Gloucester National Park, where Dad wimped out of climbing the 200-foot-high lookout tree; and Augusta in Cape Leeuwin on the furthest southwest corner of the Australian continent. We found a great camping spot at the mouth of the Blackwood River where we stayed four nights and explored the local area, seeing Pelicans, caves and the beautiful Hamelin Bay, before moving north through Margaret River to Yallingup.

**Day 22 (Monday 21st November) – Valley of the Giants**

**Julian:** *Away about 11.00. Still trying to improve but today spent time saying goodbye to Dianne and Jan. Scenic drive over Mount Shadforth gave some excellent views. William Bay was beautiful. White sand and protected by rocks. Good for the kids to swim in but flies eventually drove us away after a swim and walk. Helped to get two cars up a slippery slope.*

*Then on through more lush surroundings to Valley of the Giants where we had lunch. Took photo of car parked in Red Tingle tree. Nornalup – Walpole Inlet were a bit disappointing. Visibility had dropped significantly, almost as if there was a huge bushfire nearby. Went up Hilltop Rd Scenic Lookout, saw another Tingle Tree, did the Knoll Drive, saw an Eagles nest and nearly bumped into an inquisitive kookaburra. A bit fed up with sightseeing we moved on to Northcliffe. Nothing much there apart from sawmill and local pub, (bought some beer), so we moved onto Pemberton, where we arrived as usual after dark.*

*Camper van parked in the Giant Tingle Tree*

Eucalyptus jacksonii, commonly known as the red tingle, is a species of tall tree endemic to Southwest Australia and is one of the tallest trees found in the state. One specimen, known as the 'Giant Tingle Tree' is a tourist attraction in the Walpole-Nornalup National Park. Its base has been hollowed by fire and it is claimed to have the largest girth of any living eucalypt. Parking our camper van inside this tree was one of those wondrous moments in my boyhood that sticks out vividly in my memory. 'How is this possible?', I thought; 'How is there a tree large enough that we can park not just a car but a massive camper van inside it? No-one is going to believe this!'. How is Dad so dismissive? '*Took photo of car parked in Red Tingle tree.*'! Did he not understand? This was akin to man landing on the moon! I'm sure it was this experience which got me hooked on Enid

Blyton's *The Magic Faraway Tree* (of course, it helped that mum and Dad used to read this to us before bedtime).

### Day 23 (Tuesday 22nd November) – Gloucester Tree and Cascades

**Julian:** *Unfortunately, no sign of Dianne and Jan. Must have moved on further. Day was disquietingly hot and the flies atrocious. Slow to get away even though we weren't packing up. Went to tourist Bureau to get the local Gen and did some food shopping. Visited the Gloucester Tree Lookout (200 feet tall). Very disappointed in myself. Started to climb but after 10 steps got the heebie jeebies. After all they were just stakes driven into the trunk in a circular fashion and a half-hearted attempt at a wire safety cage around them. Would have been a superb view from the top.*

*Had lunch there, kids were foul, all feeling sweaty and hot. Then went to The Cascades arriving there with a puncture in the right front tyre. What with the slope and weight of baggage on the front couldn't get jack under and got even more sweaty and dusty digging a hole. Then found jack did not lift wheel high enough off the ground. After unloading whole of roof rack eventual success by playing with bricks. Many comments from hordes of school children who descended off the school bus. Enjoyable swim and walk after. Got back to camp in fairly good mood which soon melted after cutting my finger and with kids in foul mood again.*

The Gloucester Tree, a renowned karri tree named (in 1946) after the English city, served as a fire lookout. The platform and cabin 60m above the ground and climbing pegs were installed in 1947; by 1963, it was estimated that over 3,000 people had climbed the tree, and in 1973 the original wooden cabin was demolished and replaced with an aluminium and steel cabin and gallery. I'm not sure if I was in Dad's shoes, I would have made it to the top either. The Cascades, also in Gloucester National Park, is a cascade waterfall at Lefroy Brook.

### Day 24 (Wednesday 23rd November) – Augusta

**Julian:** *Got away around 11 after the usual muddle. Wanted to visit the trout* *hatcheries but they were shut due to modernisation. Passed through Manjimup, Bridgetown without stopping except for petrol. Nothing much to see and we wanted to camp on the coast again. Had lunch on a forest track and reached Augusta about 4:30. Plenty of time for an early evening we thought but after five hours of changing the gas cylinder and then preparing beer goulash in the pressure cooker we went to bed feeling a bit fed up.*

### Day 25 (Thursday 24th November) – Pelicans, caves and Hamelin Bay

**Julian:** *Lovely camping spot near the mouth of the Blackwood River, quiet with people pottering around doing their own thing, mainly fishing. Spent a quiet morning clearing up and watching the Pelicans. They gather there to grab scraps from the fishermen. About midday left to find Jewel Cave. Arrived there early so had picnic lunch. A really beautiful huge cave. Stalagmites, stalagmites, helictites, waterfalls and really long straws.*

*A few kilometres on to Hamelin Bay, a beautiful expanse of white sand with surf pounding in. Built a huge sandcastle with a moat which was soon awash with the incoming tide. What with the tide and the children it was soon flattened. Returned to camp and cooked chops on barbeque. Met couple with Suzuki and caravan with two kids who we had helped the day before when they ran out of petrol. Helped us cook supper.*

### Day 26 (Friday 25th November) – Mum's first fish

**Becky:** *Had a gorgeous day, though did not start propitiously. I hauled the washing off to the washroom and spent three or four hours over the twin tub. Felt really pleased when all was done, including sheepskin. Had a lovely lunch and wandered off to the jetty with James and Mark to do some fishing (first time ever for me). Kids had been so excited they had they had helped with the washing. Well, we sat there perhaps for an hour, and I caught one at least five or six inches big. Kids were as thrilled as I was.*

*Jules was back at camp fixing the seat that some heavy body had bust. He wasn't particularly keen to fish; must admit I had some pangs while it wriggled in the bucket. We went off to Leeuwin Lighthouse, viewed the Sothern and Indian Oceans and returned for tea, steak stew and grilled fish. Decided to stay another day to catch up on bits and pieces. Andrew still waking two or three times per night.*

*Mum caught her first fish*

*Mum chilling in her flares*

*Cute little brothers*

**Day 27 (Saturday 26th November) – Cleaning, sorting and fishing**

**Julian:** *Decided to stay yet another day at Turner Park Augusta. Lazy day sunning ourselves. A bit of spring cleaning on the car. Took carpet out and* *spray cleaned it. Slight improvement. James and Mark went out fishing with a couple camping next door. They had them both in the morning and afternoon and gave us some breathing space. Interesting fellow who had travelled a lot as a Mercenary and then become an oil rig engineer. Recently retired and married, they appeared to love children. James caught two fish in the morning and Mark one in the afternoon. A small walk in the afternoon for us and then back for more barbequed steak. Worked late into the night sorting out clothes and putting carpet back.*

## Day 28 (Sunday 27th November) – Lost wallet

**Julian:** *A disappointing start to the day. Even though everything had seemed sorted out from our toils of the evening before, nothing seemed to go smoothly. Kids and us were in a foul mood (Becky had a tantrum). Eventually got away about 12:30. While buying pies for lunch we discovered we could not find our wallet which had about $150 in it. No sign of it back at the camp. However, we resigned ourselves to it having been stolen and set off up Caves Road towards Margaret River. Borannup Scenic Drive was beautiful and put us in a better mood. Then went on to Lake Cave but unfortunately missed the last tour which was at 1:30 PM. Visited Mammoth Cave just along the way. Interesting fossil remains but not so impressive as Jewel. Girl guide not very sure of her facts and spoke quietly. Quite impossible to hear against Peter's natter. On towards Yallingup where we camped at Canal Rocks on the coast.*

Chapter Five

# Yallingup to Perth

*Monday 28th November – Sunday 4th December*

For thousands of years, the Indian Ocean has carved crevasses and channels into the rocks of the headland at Yallingup, forming a network of patchy rocky islands and a canal after which Canal Rocks is named. While today a footbridge allows visitors to access the rocks themselves, in 1977 we contented ourselves with visits to the Old Mill, run by a couple from Dad's hometown of Farnham, England, the spectacular Yallingup Cave and stunning Geographe Bay. A couple of nights on the beachfront at a nice campsite in Dunsborough and we saw Dad's 33rd birthday in on 30th November before heading on to Bunbury for a night and then onto Perth, our final stop before leaving Australia for Southeast Asia.

### Day 29 (Monday 28th November) – The Old Mill and Yallingup Cave

**Julian:** *Not a very pleasant place to camp. Very dry and stony and looking rather derelict. Could have been quite good if some care had been taken. Loud blaring music sent us nearly potty while clearing up. Kids did some work* [I think Dad means homework – I don't remember doing a lot of this!] *and we were away by 11.00. First visit, The Old Mill. Only old mill left standing in Australia. The water wheel was constructed to provide power for a sawmill. Couple from Farnham ran the place who had come out 11 years previously. He used to be the Blacksmith in Farnham and his wife used to work in a pub* *somewhere near the new roundabout outside Farnham.* [Near to where my father grew up in Surrey.]

*Then onto Yallingup Cave. Really beautiful with winding walkways and narrow crevices. One particular diversion, called The Crawl, had one wondering whether one would be stuck there forever. One literally had to crawl on hands and feet for about 15 feet. Made one wonder what it must have been like when it was discovered just with torchlight. Had a look around Yallingup which had impressive coastal scenery. Had a peep at Cape Naturaliste and lighthouse, (unimpressive), and stopped for a short while at Geographe Bay (Bunker Bay). Beautiful minute shells and we thought we might return there the next day, so we camped at Greenacres Caravan Park at Dunsborough. Rather nice spot by ourselves under some trees on the beach front.*

According to Bussleton-Dunsborough Mail, as of 2018 at least, the Merifield family still owned the Old Mill at Yallingup and have done since 1976, so they owned the place when we arrived at the end of 1977. Brother and sister Brett and Letitia Merifield were given planning permission to set up a wedding venue business in 2018.

*The Old Mill, Yallingup, owned by the ex-Blacksmith from Farnham in Surrey, England*

42

Geographe Bay looks stunning. Westernaustralia.com describes it as follows: 'Busselton's seaside suburb of Geographe sits on the long curve of beautiful Geographe Bay boasting sweeping Indian Ocean views, white sand beaches and calm turquoise waters. It's also just minutes from the centre of Busselton – twice crowned Western Australia's Top Tourism Town – and a short hop from the world-renowned Margaret River wine region.'

Greenacres Caravan Park was sold as prime beachfront real estate in 1998; not for lack of custom apparently, as you had to book up a year in advance. It was a popular surfing venue in the 60's and 70's. The site is now home to the Regency Beach Club.

### Day 30 (Tuesday 29th November) – Canoe

**Julian:** *Lazy day catching up. Blew canoe up and mucked about on the water. Good spot for the kids as water was shallow for a long way out.*

*I thought this was the coolest canoe ever*

*Walked into town with all the kids in the afternoon and bought $20 worth of food. Rotten stewing steak which took hours to cut up for tea. Very late again. Never did return to Bunkers Bay.*

## Day 31 (Wednesday 30th November) – Dad's Birthday and 'Sexy Boppam'

**Julian:** *Big wash and pack up in morning. My birthday and I got an 'Overlander' from the kids and a beautiful leather wallet from Beck. Did not get away until 2pm. What a record! Did not think much of Busselton, supposedly the tourist spot of the South with 19 caravan parks and the second longest jetty in Australia. Oh! Before leaving Dunsborough I had to park in a very specific manner in order for Beck to load on some very special goods, I wonder what? Missed out on some historic house as we were too late but saw replica of old school and single teachers' house.*

*Went on to Bunbury – quite an industrial town. The tourist guide tried to sell us a campsite surrounded by cranes, railways, conveyor belts and towers with no shade. No go, we returned to the only other campsite on the other side of town. $5 – we were shocked, [$3-4* was the norm] *but we did have some shade. More furtive activities at the rear of the van while unpacking. Kids went off to watch television. Very organised and we soon had tea out of the way. More furtive activities and striking of matches in the tent and in walks a beautiful birthday cake covered in 33 candles. We all got stuck in and went to bed feeling in a good mood, but not before the kids had been corrupted by a pornographic film showing at the Drive-In next door. Pete went to bed shouting 'Sexy Boppam'.*

The Overlander was a monthly magazine about travelling with lots of tips and advice. There were quite a lot of people travelling in Asia at this time. I was amused to hear that $5 AUD (equivalent to $30 today) was shocking to my Dad to camp for a night in 1977; they were used to paying $3-4 ($18-24). I love the description of Mum's 'furtive activities', and the appearance of Dad's 33rd birthday cake. It drives home how incredibly young they were to be undertaking such an enormous adventure with four kids. Most of us haven't even had our first child by 33 these days!

The consensus amongst my brothers and father is that I taught my younger brother Pete to say 'Sexy Boppam'. I suppose it could have been me. I have a vague memory of Mark, Pete and I being tucked up in our sleeping bags in the camper van roof bed. In my mind's eye we were able to see the large screen of the Drive-In next door very clearly through our mosquito screen windows, (with the Velcro curtains down), and we giggled uncontrollably. Quite a night!

## Day 32 (Thursday 1st December) – Perth

**Julian:** *Unfortunately, the only worthwhile thing to do in Bunbury, the steam train, was not operating, so we decided to push straight onto Perth. Three hours later we got our first sight of the impressive Perth skyline as we entered via the causeway over the Swan River. Clean, friendly people and well dressed. After asking directions a few times, we made our way to the Post Office where we collected a pile of mail. Dianne had decided to come on the Little Tour. Now where to camp? Got thoroughly lost and decided to follow the sun west towards the coast. Then tried campsite after campsite, all without proper shade. Eventually, absolutely exhausted and fed up we arrived at Wesnova. Two half pitchings of the tent later, in different spots of course, we found ourselves installed in a caravan for $44 a week.*

Perth's skyline was particularly impressive after travelling 2,287 miles across Australia, not having seen another city since leaving Adelaide two months earlier. Perth is the world's most isolated capital city (of Western Australia), Australia's fourth largest, and home to over 2.1 million people in 2023. It's population has more than doubled from 864,000 when we arrived on 1st December 1977, being one of the most desirable cities in the world. The city, named after Perth in Scotland, was founded by Captain James Stirling in 1829 as the administrative centre of the Swan River Colony.

## Day 33 (Friday 2nd December) – Paperwork

**Julian:** *Completely unpacked car in morning and I set off for town for a frustrating morning. Phoned pay office and found I had just been paid $3,200 back pay. Eventually got through to Clem, no Group Certificate [insurance] yet. Went to bank, money not yet in my bank account. All this took the whole morning. Returned to camp, getting really hot, had a swim and returned to*

*Perth. Visited RAC and then a walk around a park.*

### Days 34-35 (Saturday 3rd to Sunday 4th December) – Sorting and swimming

**Julian:** *A quiet weekend sorting and swimming. Weather heating up. Met Lynn on the Saturday, who immediately got interested in coming overland with us. On Sunday drove down to Freemantle and spent a while looking around Coogee Beach and campsite. Quite impressed apart from the argumentative tubby little lass who got annoyed when we told her she was driving too fast. Thousands of boats on the Swan River make a really impressive and beautiful sight.*

# Chapter Six

# Perth Preparations

*Monday 5th – Sunday 11th December*

It sounds like Dad was a bit stressed this week. And in such a state, of course everything is bound to go wrong – no flights to Bali, Pete poohing his pants in the travel agency, stifling summer heat, and no suitable berths on, the *Centaur*, the ship which was taking our camper van to Singapore. How frustrating it must have been when Mum just waltzed into the first travel agency she saw and booked six flight tickets to Bali for Christmas! $16 on photographs sounds expensive for 1977, but I'm so glad they took so many, as I doubt this book would have been possible otherwise. The highlight of the week must have been going to the cinema to see Star Wars, not that I have any recollection of seeing it!

**Julian:** *This week was rather hectic and as a consequence the diary got rather neglected. I saw Peter Hannan, the overseas motoring fellow, first thing Monday morning at the RAC, then down to Freemantle to see a Laurie Dunkly at the shipping agents. Unfortunately, the 'Jasper Nova' was not to sail until 31st of December. The real disappointment was when I went to the Indonesian travel centre and there was only one Qantas flight to Bali per week and these were booked until mid Jan. Peter poohed his pants in the travel centre.*

*The whole week was stiflingly hot. Tuesday especially, and we spent the day by the pool with the odd excursion to the telephone booth to phone Peter Hannan and*

*Laurie Dunkly. I was trying to find out whether we could cruise to Singapore as Bali seemed out. And to know, again, would it be beneficial to accompany the van on the passenger ship Centaur at the higher cargo rate. Apparently not.*

*Wednesday, we went into town late. I enquired about berths on the Centaur but apparently these were pretty booked, and we would have had to be separated. Of course, I then went to meet Becky with this further disappointing news only to find that she had walked straight into the first travel agent she had seen and booked six tickets to Bali! Thursday, we went into town early and sorted out all the details with the travel agent, having first spent $16 on photographs. In the afternoon Beck stayed at the campsite with the kids and I went down to Fremantle to confirm the booking of the van on the Jasper Nova. Spent well over $2,000 that day.*

*Weather continued to be hot, and the caravan got stifling during the day. We decided to stay one more night and then move over to the camping ground and some shade. That night, Lynn kindly babysat for us, and we took James and Mark to see Star Wars. It must have been the night before, Wednesday night, that we first met Penny and Helen who had recently come over from England driving a combi. They gave us some helpful hints that night and after. Coming back from the pictures Thursday night we very nearly ran out of petrol. That really would have been ironical.*

*Saturday 10th December – me at Swan River*

*At the Park in Perth*

*Star Wars*, 1977 – the first of the most celebrated Sci-Fi Saga of all time – was not always destined for such fame in the minds of the original cast and crew. Production difficulties during filming on location including Tunisia and Elstree Studios in England, meant the film went $3m over budget and most thought it would be a flop. Released in May 1977 in a few select US cinemas, it immediately became a runaway success, much to the surprise of its creators. By the time it was released in Australia on 27th October 1977, *Star Wars* was gaining cult status. I am therefore surprised I have no recollection of going to see the film at all. The original version we saw in Australia was censored – with the scene cut depicting the smouldering bodies of Luke Skywalker's aunt and uncle after a stormtrooper attack. They needn't have done this on my behalf – after the whaling station, I could stomach anything! Today's version includes the scene and is rated PG.

**Julian:** *Friday, another stifling day, we spent packing up, cleaning the caravan and moving over to the campsite. Pitched the tent right under a tree. Beautiful shade. Late afternoon we drove with Lynn to Kings Park. Kids were grotty that night. Over tired. Saturday, Lynn moved out to go to Sorento Caravan*

*Park. Saturday afternoon went for a drive in the hills. No cooler there so went swimming on the Swan River. Becky slept most of the afternoon, at least until tea was served. Sunday was the day of the parade. Again, hot and thousands of people. Did not get a very good view.*

I tried in vain to find details on the internet of the parade Dad mentions on Sunday 11th December. Despite his less than keen description I am intrigued and would love to know more. I thought you could find anything out on the internet these days, but apparently not ...

# PART II
# BALI & SINGAPORE
## *(2787 miles)*

~

*Bali*

Map © 2025 Google

Chapter Seven

# Perth to Bali

*Monday 12th – Sunday 18th December*

M ore preparations for our Asia trip this week; up until our flight to Bali on Saturday 17th December. A sheepskin seat cover, 'Gaz' cylinders, tent waterproofing, sunshades, a lockable petrol cap, spare tent and a new trunk (to replace the one which had blown off the roof at Twilight Cove). All this shopping meant we ran out of money, leading to an embarrassing moment in a shop and a disagreement between Mum and Dad. I think the pressure of finally leaving familiar Australia for more foreign climes was building up. Dad dropped the camper at the port in 40°C heat, leaving the rest of us at the Flag Motor Lodge in air-conditioned comfort, and took the train back. The next day we were off to Bali where we were reunited with Dianne, who introduced us to a very different way of life...

**Days 43-46 (Monday 12th to Thursday 15th December) – Provisioning**

**Julian:** *Again, this week the diary was rather neglected as we were still rushing around trying to get the last things tied up. Monday, I took the two older kids to town. Got spare parts at Toyota and went to see Peter Hannan again. Got an expensive sheepskin for the centre seat and 'Trans Asia Motoring' and then to the Post office.*

*Peter had given me an address where we could pick up some discarded GAZ cylinders, so on the Tuesday we all went to town. Becky cashed her child* *endowment, we get out at Hungry Jacks and while Beck went looking for schoolbooks, I went off and bought a couple of GAZ cylinders for $4. We met again at the camping shop and bought waterproofing for the tent. Then up to north Perth to find a baby shop where we bought 2 sunshades, one for the pram and one for the pushchair. Unfortunately, we were too late to have a fitting made up for the GAZ cylinders.*

It sounds like discarded GAZ cylinders at $4 a pop was a good deal (which Dad would have loved). 'GAZ' or bottled LPG was our camper van's cooking fuel. It was such an important aspect of our lives, featuring several times in the trip diary, it is worthy of a few words. Apparently, the LPG industry began in America in 1910, when a motorist noticing his car's gasoline was evaporating wanted it investigated. This resulted in a government chemist separating butane and propane, the combination of which was later used to power a farm in Pennsylvania on 17th May, 1912 – the birthday of LPG. LPG came to Australia 24 years later in 1936 when Bill Dunlop, (the first boss of Ampol), showed Ernie Steventon, (a Sydney motor mechanic), the flame from a LPG cylinder, saying: 'You ought to get out of the motor garage business and distribute this. It's the up-and-coming fuel of the future.' In typical 'just do it' Aussie fashion, Steventon took up the challenge: first selling imported US gas to caravan owners, then securing a local supply and even making his own equipment and appliances.

**Julian:** *Next day Wednesday, I went back to north Perth to arrange the gas fitting, then to town. Bought a locking petrol cap for the spare tank and on way home some STP* [presumably sealant tape]. *In afternoon waterproofed the tent but only managed to do the roof and front side with three tins. Sometime in the last few the days we had also invested in a new tent for the boys and a new trunk.*

*Next morning the car went in for a service at Maida Vale. Then to town – still no tickets and no passport and I needed to cash money. Luckily the travel agent phoned American Express and explained the situation and I was able to cash some travellers cheques. Becky went off to buy more waterproofing for the tent and I went to change the headlight at Toyota. Up to Kings Park where we got Andrew's last polio done and then back along Guildford Road. Tried to stock up on stores but ran out of money and had an 'Argy Bargy' with Beck. She was quite rude to me in front of everyone! On the way back got rid of masses of change at the bottle shop buying drinks for a booze up tonight. All a wee bit tired so it really wasn't much of a party.*

**Becky:** *He damn well deserved it too! Got enough stuff for trip – baby food dried milk etc. He refused to give me any more money. Really embarrassing giving back all the goods; now we haven't enough, especially for the baby.*

I can just picture it – Mum was not to be trifled with, so Dad was either being very foolhardy or brave in refusing her any more money. Given we clearly needed the baby food for the trip, perhaps in hindsight Dad, it may have been best to hand over the 'masses of change' you were hoarding for the booze? Another thing which strikes me from this entry is the number of UK place names – Perth, Maida Vale, Guildford Road. Not so surprising perhaps, given that Australia was originally a British colony, but in a wider context, (yesterday I was cycling in Woking Road in Wessex Estate in Singapore), it is a constant mystery to me that such a small island in northern Europe could have such a global impact. Being from Surrey, the proliferation of Surrey place names in so many countries feel strange yet somehow comforting.

### Day 47 (Friday 16th December) – Final preparations

**Julian:** *One hell of a day – again boiling hot. Forecast 40°C – typical! Got up early. The camper needed complete reorganisation and with everything off the roof rack it was one hell of a squeeze inside the camper when we eventually set off around 2pm. First stop the Flag Inn Motel where we offloaded nearly half the junk to take to Bali. While the kids and Beck were deported in air-conditioned comfort and television, I set off again into the blazing sun. Collected the tickets, visas, passports etc, encashed more travellers cheques and checked at the post office. One card from Sue Patterson telling us to get on our way. Then up north to collect the GAZ fitting ($15). Five to four I was supposed to be at Fremantle* *at 4:00 PM. A mad rush down there. Got there 4.45. Luckily Laurie Dunkley was still there. Sorted out the last few details, gave her $25 and went to see George at the next door garage. Another complete reorganisation of the camper so George would be able to get at the battery. Then a walk to the station and back to the motel by taxi. A relatively relaxing evening; cooked our own steaks in the restaurant and watched 'Space' on television.*

The Flag Motor Lodge opened its doors in 1967, offering modern and stylish accommodation from just $7 per night. Ten years later when we arrived for our last night in Australia, the motel had undergone its first major renovation, in 1975, with the addition of superior, self-catering rooms, in whose 'air-conditioned comfort and television' we were deported, whilst Dad ventured forth into the 'blazing sun'. AC was a relatively new, but very welcome, development in Australia at the time.

Most homes in Australia still did not have AC, so our motel room with its iconic 70's mustard and brown colour scheme would have indeed seemed luxurious, especially after slumming it for 7 weeks in the camper (quite so at $48!). It doesn't make the diary, but I recall the swimming pool where I was stung by a bee on our last day, (I expect Andy's impetigo spots were more concerning). It must have been quite a relief for Mum and Dad to get on that plane to Bali after the mad rush of the last few days.

**Day 48 (Saturday 17th December) – Departure Day**

**Julian:** *Mercurochrome and Panadol on the carpet followed by breakfast in our room. We had asked to stay until 12 so we weren't too hassled. Andrew had nasty looking impetigo spots, so I walked down to nearby chemist for some Erythramycin and Neasporin cream. Just as I arrived back, Mike Booth and family arrived. Their Land Rover was going over on the same boat and they were flying to Singapore in a week's time. Coffee for all and then Lynn plus husband arrived. Seems quite a nice chap who helped us a lot. Mad last-minute rush packing and labelling the bags and off to the airport in Lynn's van. Motel had cost us $48 in all. Met the girls at the airport and checked in. Eventually after a lot of hassles got ourselves onto a Boeing 707, bassinet and all. 3 ½ hours* *to Bali, clocks went back 1 hr. Quite pleased with the service on the plane.*

*Really humid and cloudy at the other end. Long wait to get through health check, passport control and customs. Besieged at other end by porters. Luckily Dianne was there and we were really glad to see her. Then many others besieged us offering us cheap accommodation. Eventually got away to Kuta in a Bemo. Did not like Sapta Petala so went to another losmen in the centre of town for 1,000 Rupiahs for two rooms. Very basic and a bit grotty and our first experience of an Asian loo. Charming people though. Dianne took us out to a bar type restaurant and we had our first experience of Indonesian food with iced lemon and iced chocolate. Everyone very friendly and interested in the children. I was fascinated by the completely different mode of life. Very humid and we went to bed exhausted and sweating.*

The 'girls' were friends of Dianne, who she had met on the plane. In a letter home on Dec 11th from Darwin before her flight to Bali the next day, Dianne writes 'everything has worked out with the Littles; they leave for Bali on Dec 17th so hope to see them then'.

Her next letter said 'Staying at losman (pension) at Kuta Beach – cost 300 rp night (75cents) so really cheap but very basic – shower is a well of water and bucket and toilet is hole in the ground. Have been travelling by local transport so far – *bemos* – they are really covered pickup trucks so very bumpy rides. The Littles arrive tomorrow – will be glad to see them again. Probably stay with them until Wed then head for Java'.

The next letter said 'The Littles arrived yesterday – really funny to be travelling with them – everyone stares at you – not often they see a typical English family with pram walking down the streets of Kuta! We are all going into the mountains for 2 days tomorrow'.

Today Kuta Beach where we stayed in Bali is a major tourist destination, especially for Australians, but back in the 1970's it was just getting going. As such and as Dianne describes, we were a novelty to the locals – Mum, Dad and four blonde boys, one in a pram. This was our first experience of what was to become a recurring theme during our Asia leg. Kuta was also the site of the horrific Bali Bombings in 2002, 25 years after our stay. 88 Australians, 38 Indonesians and 23 Britons, as well as 53 more people from over 20 nationalities were killed, mainly in their 20s and 30s. The first bomb was detonated at 11.05pm on 12th October, one of the busiest tourist periods of the year, by a suicide bomber with a backpack inside Paddy's Pub. This caused many to flee into the street, where 20 seconds later another suicide bomber detonated a second much more powerful bomb inside a car parked just opposite Paddy's. Jemaah Islamiyah, a violent Islamist group was found to be responsible. Three members were sentenced to death and executed by firing squad less than a month later.

### Day 49 (Sunday 18th December) – Waking up in Bali

**Julian:** *Everyone wakes early in Bali even if you don't want to. The cockerels see to that. Well after a squat and scoop in the loo we had breakfast of bananas and strained tea from a thermos flask. We were to get really sick of that thermos flask tea by the time we left Bali. Off to beach with all our gear. Prams are rarely seen in Bali. Great interest in the children. Then the siege of people on the beach trying to sell us things. Bought a two-piece dress for Beck, a shirt and some shorts for me and two t-shirts for the boys. I'm sure we were done.*

*The heat was soon too much so off to the eating house at the end of the main street by the beach. More ice lemons and ice chocolates and a sample of Indonesian food. Met Dianne there, had a further swim and then back to her losmen. She had booked a two-day trip for the next day.*

*We met the other girls who were going to the Kecak dance that night. Unfortunately, we never made it – too tired. After eating we got there at the end of the performance just as they were all coming out. We had in fact heard the exciting chant 'Kecak Kecak'. There were in fact going to be two free rooms at the girls losmen so we got a few of them to come back and take several articles of rubbish back with them.*

There was no running water in our losmen, so we had to drag water up from a well in a bucket. Quite a change from the Flag Motel! Breakfasts were always the same – bananas and black tea in a thermos included in the price. The 'Kecak' dance is a Balinese Hindu dance and music drama that was developed in the 1930s. The dance is based on the story of the Ramayana and is traditionally performed by a circle of as many as 150 men in temples and villages across Bali. Also known as the Ramayana monkey chant, performers wear checked cloths around their waists, percussively chanting 'kecak' whilst moving their hands and arms. The performance depicts a battle from the Ramayana, in which the monkey-like Vanaras, led by Hanuman, help Prince Rama fight the evil King Ravana. Kecak has roots in sanghyang, a trance-inducing exorcism dance.

# Chapter Eight
# Bali
### *Monday 19th – Sunday 25th December*

This week's entry is written on Christmas Day 2022 and takes us up to this day 45 years ago. We had intended to go to Kuta, Bali so I could write from where we actually were at the time, but the rainy season didn't much appeal, so my wife Jess and I have plumbed for Krabi, Thailand, where we are scuba diving. Bit of a different Christmas for us and we are missing our sons terribly; though not too terribly…

*This week's diary write up*

### Day 50 (Monday 19th December) – Bali road trip

**Julian:** *Bananas and tea again! At last the cake man came. 50 Rupiahs for 1 and 350 for 6!! We had got early breakfast and got over to Daine's by 7am! Seven of us plus 4 children plus 2 drivers piled into a Datsun van about the same size as the Toyota.*

*'The Girls' with guide*

*More stops en route*

*Me tickling Peter*

*We passed through numerous villages where they carried out wood carving or working gold and silver into jewellery. Also saw Barong-Kris dance. Wherever we stopped we were immediately surrounded and the kids taken over. Although village life was very basic and had been carried on as such for thousands of years, we never saw any real poverty. Everything seemed clean and neat, an impression that was to be shattered when I went to Denpasar. Fascinating to see the country people about their daily work harvesting rice, selling their wares in the market.*

*Then we started to climb. Stopped at a very expensive restaurant with beautiful views especially for the tourist but too expensive to eat or even drink at. Carried on up to village and holy temple Besakih on Mount Ganung Agung. Peter had a tantrum and poohed his pants in the temple. Then on descending and climbing until we reached Penelokan where we were to stay. What a magnificent view looking over a valley to Mount Ganung Batur with its smoking crater mingling with the clouds and Batur Lake lying at its feet.*

*The losmen was however filthy and I'm sure fleas were in the bed. We as a family got a single room with two single beds and a hole at the back that stunk us out all night. It seemed that the lady of the losmen was trying to pack as many people as possible into the place. Bodies all over the floor. As darkness settled in, the losmen became completely enveloped in cloud and the rain pelted down. Met a fellow called Peter there. Kids played chess with him. Quite a homely community feeling about the place. A wee bit chilly so we all wrapped up well for the night.*

Dad mentions Mount Agung, an active volcano, which erupted in March 1963 with devastating consequences, destroying villages and killing an estimated 1,500 people. Lahars, (mudflows composed of pyroclastic material caused by heavy rainfall), killed an additional 200 people and minor eruptions and flows followed, lasting almost a year. Between 2017-2019, the area experienced further earthquakes and further volcanic activity. Over 100,000 people were evacuated from their homes. Successive eruptions caused ash clouds which interfered with air traffic and stranded tourists, and one of which spewed lava and rocks over 3 km, with some ash falling on nearby villages. Thankfully there were no deaths, but the activity severely affected tourism, which is the main economic activity in the area.

My wife and I, and two sons Thomas and George, came on a scuba diving holiday to Amed, in the same area, for Easter 2023. On enquiring about the eruptions, local people were at pains to tell us how safe it is now. Not surprising after the double whammy of the further eruptions followed by two years of COVID 19! Thankfully, we felt no eruptions or earthquakes, the people were friendly and welcoming, the landscape beautiful, and the sea life incredibly rich and vibrant – no doubt because of the fertile volcanic sand which, unsurprisingly, is black. A stark reminder of the fragile balance of life on our beautiful, dangerous planet.

### Day 51 (Tuesday 20th December) – Black beaches and Monkey Temple

**Julian:** *A lovely morning. Off at 8:00 AM. Most people had had a cold restless night's sleep. A long descent to the northern coast where we had a paddle and a drink. The sand there was black. Passed through Singaraja which seemed quite a large bustling place. Back up over the mountains along another road. Stopped for lunch at a small village with a temple and a lake. Then onto the Monkey Temple at Mengwi where Peter had the shock of his life when a monkey snatched some nuts out of his hand. Stopped at Denpasar for letters but PO was shut. Arrived exhausted back at our new losmen, had a quiet meal out at the Daggies and retired to bed.*

*My family on Amed Beach in 2023, with Mount Agung in the background*

The name Singaraja means 'Lion King' and the town is the second largest on the island. It used to be the largest, as the Dutch colonial capital of Bali from 1849 until Indonesian independence in 1948 and remained capital until 1958. Singaraja was the administrative centre and port of arrival for most visitors to Bali until the 1960's when the Bukit Peninsula in the south became more developed, after Denpasar became the new capital. The town houses the only library of Lontar Manuscripts, which are made from dried palm leaves, in the world. Some date back to the 5th century BCE and their use continued until printing presses replaced hand-written manuscripts in the 19th century.

Text was inscribed with a pen knife after which colourings were applied and then wiped off, leaving the ink in the grooves. The sheets were typically held together by a string which was passed through a hole in each sheet, resulting in a rather beautiful fan effect. The term 'Lontar' is specific to the Indonesian palm leaf manuscripts; it means leaf of the Palmyra palm, which are also known as 'fan trees', due to the shape of the leaves. Today, Balinese Brahmin still write in *rontal*, which is performed as a sacred duty to rewrite Hindu texts.

### Day 52 (Wednesday 21st December) – Back at Kuta Beach

**Julian:** *Lazy day settling ourselves in. Few hours down at the beach but too hot to stay there for long. Magnificent waves for surfing. Kids loved it. Even Peter got quite used to being splashed in the face. However he always hated the scoop used for washing, but the water was a damned sight colder than the sea. The losmen was very clean.*

*Back at Kuta Beach*

**Becky:** *Actually, I've just remembered I was very sick that day with throbbing head, temperature, and touch of diarrhoea, in spite of heat after a morning walk. I collapsed and slept several hours in our new, clean losmen. Didn't eat that night nor did kids, all went to bed early and slept well.*

Dad mentions '*Magnificent waves for surfing*', (perhaps a little wistfully). Surfing became popular in Bali in the late 60s and early 70s, especially following Albert Falzon's classic surfing film *Morning of the Earth*, the first to capture surfing in Bali. Its two surfers, Stephen Cooney and Rusty Miller, became the first to ever surf the now world-famous point break, Uluwatu, in Bali's extreme southwest. This iconic film premiered in Sydney in 1972 and instantly became a hit at the box office. It tells the story of surfers living in spiritual harmony with nature, making their own boards (and homes) as they travelled in search of the perfect wave across Australia's north-east coast, Bali and Hawaii. It's alternative approach and legendry country-soul soundtrack by G.Wayne Thomas, combined with an inspiring story and stunning visuals resonated deeply with Australia's youth and cemented the film as a national treasure.

The release of the film coincided with and is often attributed for the rise of Bali as a major tourist destination. Surfing is now a multimillion-dollar industry in Bali, accounting for around 10% of all tourism revenue. I bet you were itching to get out there with those surfers weren't you Dad!

### Day 53 (Thursday 22nd December) – Making friends

**Becky:** *Still felt a bit grotty but got up and went for a walk with kids, again another lazy day didn't do very much. Still very sticky. Had cat nap very late in afternoon, Peter been a bit irritable lately. We all went for a meal up the road where we met a New Zealand chap and his two boys, three and six, who really liked Bali. We chatted to him and two other Americans who had nearly had to rescue us the night before as we thought we'd no money left to pay the bill having paid 70,000 Rupiahs for the mountain trip, the drivers of whom looked extremely pleased when given their dues?? Eventually retired. Andrew now sleeps in our bed and disturbs us far less (only two or three times and then only me). His pram must be hot. What a nuisance, he settles less and less comfortably in it each day.*

### Day 54 (Friday 23rd December) – Farewell girls

**Becky:** *Today all the girls we met through Dianne plus her, left for Jakarta. Dianne shuffled off early while I was in the shower much to my disgust. We lounged around having a quiet day and a nice meal in the evening. Feel generally a bit more cheerful. Kerry, Judy and Kerry's grandma left in the afternoon; very friendly.*

**Julian:** *I went to Denpasar. Horrible noisy place with masses of hooting motorcycles and garbage everywhere. Post office closed.*

### Day 55 (Saturday 24th December) – Water and washing on Christmas Eve

**Becky:** *Today Julian and I still feeling cheerful. We scrubbed washing together and hoiked our water from the well. It's amazing how little water you manage with when you have to.*

**Julian:** *It was either Friday or Saturday night we went to Legian to see the monkey dance. In morning again went to Denpasar but no post.*

### Day 56 (Sunday 25th December) – Christmas Day

**Julian:** *Christmas day. Who would have known it. Certainly didn't feel like it. More washing in the morning. Again, very hot. There were many restaurants doing Christmas dinners for the tourist but they seemed very expensive and a bit of an exploitation. We ended up, much to Beck's disappointment, in a small quiet restaurant where the chicken which they offered was 'off'. And the satay they offered was 'off'. I think Beck was feeling rather homesick. Anyway, we had beef steak and prawns and Christmas cake (Jianne's and very rich) and laced our coffee with a bottle of Johnnie Walkers I had splashed out on the day before. The people seemed very friendly, and we decided to go back there the next night to try chicken with Almonds.*

Jianne was a good friend of Mum's back in Australia, and she had kindly baked this cake for us to have on Christmas Day. Dad doesn't write about it, but I remember being on the beach and feeling really chuffed with my present of a miniature boxed book set of Peter Rabbit stories.

# Chapter Nine
# Bali to Singapore
*Monday 26th December – Sunday 1st January 1978*

Singapore, our next destination, and where Jess and I now live, is a small island located at the tip of the Malay Peninsula between the Pacific and Indian Oceans. According to Malay legend a Srivijayan prince of Palembang (Sumatra), Sang Nila Utama, landed on the island on a hunting trip in the 13th Century and spotting what he thought was a lion, founded a settlement called Singapura, meaning 'Lion City' in Sanskrit. The truth of this sighting is dubious to say the least. Lions have never been found near the dense forests of the equatorial tropics – they prefer the open, dry habitat of woodland savannas and the furthest east lions have been known is in Gujarat in western India, 3000km from Singapore. Nevertheless, the lion symbolised power and respect, in India being a royal creature associated with kings. As Indian culture expanded eastwards the lion grew in cultural significance, if not in actual presence, with at least three other places in Southeast Asia named after lions. Assuming Sang Nila Utama did indeed see a creature which he took to be a lion, it is in fact much more likely to have been an Asian golden cat.

Singapore's strategic location, and the presence of a sheltered port make it the perfect trading post and there is evidence of it being an important trading settlement as early as the 14th Century. Today Singapore is the world's busiest transhipment port and second busiest in terms of shipping tonnage, (surpassed by Shanghai in 2010), handling a fifth of all container transhipments and half of all crude oil shipments.

This tiny island, 743km2, was variously ruled by the Malacca and Johor Sultanates in what is today modern-day Malaysia. In 1819, Stamford Raffles, a British statesman negotiated a treaty with Johor, allowing the British to locate a trading port on the island to compete with the Dutch who dominated trade in the region and whose stronghold was Batavia, now Jakarta. This led to Singapore being established as a British colony in 1867. At the time Singapore had an estimated population of around 1,000 people, mainly Malays, with a handful of Chinese. By 1871 this had reached 100,000, over half Chinese, many of whom came to work in the plantations and tin mines. Predominantly male, most returned home to China, India, Malaya and other parts of Asia when they had earned enough money. Many, however, chose to stay permanently and their descendants now form the bulk of Singapore's citizens who at the time of writing number 3.6 million. Another 2.4 million foreign workers and dependents bring the total current population to 6 million, and the island state is today one of the most prosperous countries in the world. On our arrival in 1977 there were 2.3 million residents and Singapore was a bustling, vibrant place, full of promise.

The man most responsible for Singapore's incredible modern-day success was Lee Kuan Yew, Prime Minister from Singapore's independence in 1965 until 1990. Following the Second World War, and the invasion and occupation by Japan from 1942 to 1945, Singapore reverted to British control, whose granting of increasing levels of self-government resulted in the merger of Singapore with the Federation of Malaya, to form Malaysia in 1963. However, social unrest, racial tensions, and political differences between the governing People's Action Party (PAP) and Malaysia's Alliance Party resulted in Singapore's expulsion from Malaysia. Singapore became an independent republic on 9 August 1965, with the leader of the PAP, Lee Kuan Yew, a young Cambridge educated lawyer, becoming its first, hesitant, Prime Minister. He had believed wholeheartedly in the merger of

Malaya and Singapore with, in his words, 'people connected by geography, economics and ties of kinship'.

When it became apparent that the merger would not work, due mainly to the different racial make-up of the two territories (with Singapore's population being predominantly comprised of Chinese ethnic origin), the new republic faced an uncertain future. There was a real danger of attack by Indonesia, and of forcible re-integration into the Malaysia Federation on unfavourable terms, in addition to significant problems of unemployment, housing, education, and a lack of natural resources and land. This makes the transformation of Singapore from a beleaguered and impoverished post war British colony to a modern, independent country with a highly developed free market economy and strong international trading links, all the more astonishing.

Back to the diary and it is Boxing Day in Bali, with two more days until we fly to Singapore; the plan being to meet up with contacts of my well connected grandparents, prepare, provision and drive across the causeway to Malaysia and then all the way through Asia and Europe to England.

### Day 57 (Monday 26th December) – Siestas and sunsets

**Julian:** *I don't think we did much again. Weather really was too hot to be energetic. By this time, we had decided siestas were the thing after lunch, but it was very difficult to get Peter's and Andrew's sleep to coincide. The two older boys were fine, they usually amused themselves. It wasn't until now that we realised the best time to go to the beach was either very early morning or late afternoon. It really was rather gorgeous to sit on the sand in relative coolness and watch the sun go down over the seas. Unfortunately, it always seemed to get muggy again later on in the evening. Always incredibly warm and the beach gorgeous although perhaps not quite as good as some we had already come across in the SW of WA.*

*A very typical scene were the traders selling their wares on the beach. Jewellery, wood carvings, bikinis, drinks, shirts etc. One was forever pestered by them. They would persist and would be quite happy to sit down 1 foot from a topless*

73

*female to 'rest' Even if she had said no 100 times. Their approach to us always centred on the children. How many? All boys! They were always interested in the order. Then as if out of the blue 'would you like to see my paintings'. One always had to be on the lookout, they often tried to swindle money out of you although basically they were very honest and actual theft was not very common. That afternoon I had gone down to the travel agent see if our onward tickets had been confirmed. There was a notice on the wall saying, 'Ticket confirmation ₹500'. The chap then said, 'To you good offer, half price ₹250 per ticket, six tickets ₹1500 please'. He told me he had to go to Denpasar to confirm the tickets. After pointing out he did not have to make six journeys to Denpasar, and refusing to pay him, he said 'you very clever, alright ₹500'.*

*Bali Beach Life*

*That night we went back to the same restaurant as the night before with a girl called Sue to try the chicken with almonds. Expecting large succulent pieces of white chicken pieces mixed with rice and almonds we were confronted with this mangy looking bird with lots of bones and a little bit of brown meat thrown in, covered in a revolting looking sauce. Apparently, chickens don't thrive in Bali and are quite a treat and quite expensive. Up to now we had very little rain considering it was rainy season but that night in the restaurant the heavens really opened. Luckily it had stopped by the time we left but we still got wet wading back through several inches of water. Oh! By the way there was a hard-*

*boiled egg planted between the hind legs of this creature.*

## Day 58 (Tuesday 27th December) – Beach and rainstorm

**Julian:** *Our last full day in Bali. I woke pretty early and took James and Peter down to the beach. Really was very beautiful at this time in the morning and not too hot. Again, didn't do much. Had another siesta. Had intended taking a long walk along the beach away from town but started out too late. Sat on the beach and watched the sun go down and then walked along the beach towards town. There we found a fantastic display of shells spread out on the ground looking even more impressive in the light of numerous hurricane lamps.*

*The rain then came slowly at first but obviously the locals knew what was to come for they all started to hurriedly pack up. We got caught trying to find a suitable restaurant and took shelter under the veranda of a shop for half an hour while the water rapidly rose around us. No letting up so we decided to get drenched and sloshed on through the streets which had now turned to rivers. We eventually dripped into a restaurant and ordered hot chocolates for us all. Mark was actually complaining of being cold. Satay and beer to follow. Still pelting when we left so we got a bemo back to the losmen. We could not have been wetter had we gone into the sea with our clothes on.*

## Day 59 (Wednesday 28th December) – Off to Singapore

**Julian:** *A beautiful day. Miraculously most of the water from last night had disappeared. I again got up early and went out for last swim and took pictures of the little bamboo huts nestling under the palms in the early morning sun. Everyone else was still asleep. A last-minute clothes wash and then to Denpasar for me. We had heard there was a letter waiting for us. Peter and I collected it from the PO (Sue Patterson). Then back to Kuta for packing up. We eventually staggered away from the losmen laden to the hilt and the pram packed high with bags. The losmen had cost 11,800 RP's for eight nights, 350 for washing and 600 for five broken glasses. Sounds a lot but it won't only works out to be about $25. Luckily got a bemo to the airport. Got a shock when they asked for 5,000 RP's airport tax...*

**Becky:** *... and he got very cross, starting to lose his temper with the poor girl behind the counter. However, we managed to change some money then paid extortionate prices for drinks all around. We sat in the beautiful, air-conditioned lounge, such a luxury, and at last climbed in the plane with all our tribe only to find no bassinet and back seats. However, the trip wasn't too bad and we certainly ate well in spite of our shrunken tums. At Jakarta we noticed a plane from Vietnam being greeted with all the VIPs, a dumpy little grey suited man – never did find out who he was. Singapore was relatively hassle-free, bus to the arrival lounge, very quick through barriers. I dreaded being stopped with my Afro hairstyle and Jules' hair a bit long, but no remarks and we got a taxi to the Majestic Hotel. One large room for all of us and finally after Milos and chocolates in a nearby Chinese cafe (too late for the restaurant) we retired to bed.*

Having long hair was illegal in Singapore from the 1960's until the 1990's; it was associated with the hippie subculture and deemed by Lee Kuan Yew's government to be negative and detrimental to Singapore's development. The punishment for having long hair varied from a fine to having one's hair forcefully cut short. Government facilities were also ordered to give long-haired males the lowest priority when it came to requests for help. Long-haired male foreigners entering Singapore were requested to leave. These included the Bee Gees, Kitarō, and Led Zeppelin who all cancelled their gigs in Singapore because they refused to comply.

### Day 60 – (Thursday 29th December) – A Singapore come down

**Julian:** *This wasn't a very good introduction to Singapore. After breakfast of scrambled eggs, coffee and toast we set out to look around. We left a film to be developed and made our way to the PO via a children's playground. Letters from Grandad and Betsy. Had coffee and cakes and then started back only to get caught in teeming rain. After sheltering for half an hour with no let-up we eventually got a taxi. Arrived back at the hotel soaked.*

*In the afternoon Pete and I went off to the AA. Saw numerous sampans on the river and again got soaked. AA chap gave us a couple of addresses of shipping* *agents and told us we had to pay $30 for an import licence for the privilege of being in Singapore for 24 hours. In the morning we had tried to phone Dr Lee at his surgery with no success. Talked to Philip Day who had visitors, but he said he would contact us later.*

*That evening the restaurant was being used for a private party so we had to eat in our room. We ordered three of what we thought were small Chinese dishes and this ridiculous mammoth feast appeared before us. We were rather fed up and worried about the cost of staying in Singapore and not feeling much like eating. Two of these huge dishes were wasted and we only got through one of the two beers ordered. Went to sleep feeling rather miserable.*

A sampan is a flat-bottomed Chinese and Malay wooden boat typically propelled by oars, sometimes also with a sail, and is used for fishing and short-range transportation. Some sampans include a small shelter on board. For a time, they were virtually the only means of transporting passengers and crew between ships at anchor and the numerous landing jetties. Widely used in the heyday of economic activity, Sampans were once seen in great numbers at the Singapore River until 1983 when the river was cleared as part of Lee Kuan Yew's river clean-up campaign. As well as the removal of hundreds of tonnes of rubbish and the relocation of squatters and businesses such as pig and duck farms, some 80 discarded boats had to be removed from the Singapore, Geylang, Rochor, Serangoon and Kallang Rivers!

Dr (Alfred) Lee and Philip Day were Singapore residents – acquaintances of our grandparents, Lala and Grumpy, on my Dad's side. With Grumpy, (he was!), being a chest physician and Lala, (my older cousin coined that one as a toddler and it stuck), having grown up in South Africa and Mauritius before moving to the UK, they were well connected and provided Dad with numerous useful contacts for the trip.

### Day 61 (Friday 30th December) – Sentosa: Isle of Tranquility

**Julian:** *I was feeling really low when I woke. Had a restless night tossing and turning, really worrying whether we should go on with this trip. Luckily Philip came to the rescue and phoned to see if we wanted to go to Sentosa with them*

77

*and their friends. After breakfast in our room of toast and coffee, we got a taxi to Clifford pier and arrived there 9:15 AM. Becky dashed off to get disposable nappies. In the meantime, I met Philip, Annette and their friends, John and Jane. Beck just got back in time to jump on the boat as they were casting off. The boat took us around the harbour and gave us some good views of the skyline of Singapore and the various ship terminals. Arriving at Sentosa we boarded an old green double decker bus. We travelled around visiting the Maritime Museum, the Coralarium and the Art Centre with the Surrender Chamber attached.*

*Clifford Quay / Customs House & View from Sentosa*

Sentosa, which means 'peace and tranquillity' in Malay, is an island located 800m off the southern coast of mainland Singapore. It was initially known as Pulau Blakang Mati (Island Behind Death). From the 1880s, the island was an important British military base with several forts built on it to protect the southern shipping lanes. In 1970, the island was renamed Sentosa following a naming contest organised by the Singapore Tourist Promotion Board (STPB). The Sentosa Development Corporation (SDC), formed in 1972, was tasked with the development of the island into a tourist and recreation resort.

One of the initiatives, the brainchild of then Minister for Defence, Dr. Goh Keng Swee, was a coral garden atop Mount Serapong at the eastern end of the island; the Coralarium Dad mentions. Opened in 1974, it was the first such attraction in Asia, comprising of four acres of beautiful garden grounds with landscaped pools and coral exhibits housed in a main building, designed by the Urban Renewal Department, with the 18-metre-tall Coralon Tower. Unfortunately, this had to be dismantled in 1983 due to safety concerns over its structural stability. The surrender chamber depicted the formal Japanese surrender to the British in 1945 through wax models made by experts from Madame Tussaud's Wax Museum in London.

**Julian:** *At this time Philip realised the tour was not going to land us back at Clifford pier and started to get rather ratty with the poor woman guide. Anyway, she agreed to accompany us back to see the tour operators. We had an exciting ride back by cable car over the harbour but after seeing the organiser still no transport back to Clifford. I must say I agreed with Philip and admired him for sticking to his guns as we had received no literature telling us where the tour was taking us.*

The Singapore Cable Car connects Singapore to Sentosa. Opened in February 1974, it was one of the earliest development projects completed by the SDC, designed as both an attraction and means of transportation. Hugely popular, it drew 750,000 passengers in its first 10 months of operation. On 29 January 1983 however, tragedy struck when the derrick of a drilling ship *Eniwetok* became entangled with the cable, knocking two gondolas into the sea and killing seven passengers; the only survivor a two-year-old infant, saved from drowning by a PSA (Port of Singapore Authority) marine assistant. Thirteen more, stranded in gondolas, were rescued by two military helicopters in a nine-hour, night-time rescue operation. After months of repairs and thorough safety testing, the cable car returned to operation in August 1983. Today, after two renovations and a route extension, the cable car carries a million passengers a year, (three of whom were us, in early 2024), and is about to celebrate its 50th birthday.

**Julian:** *We split up and took a taxi back to Clifford Pier. Window shopping, refreshments and money changing in Clifford Arcade followed by a visit to the post office. No letters. Nappy changing in Raffles Place and then a trip in a rickshaw, two in fact. The leader obviously knew where he was going but it certainly wasn't back to the Majestic. Eventually after pointing out that there we were going in completely the opposite direction he said 'ooh yes' and turned around. We came to an agreement and returned to our rooms.*

*I got through then to Dr Lee and he asked us round for the evening. What troubles we had getting to the place. First, I had to explain to someone on the end of the radio where we wanted to go but even that wasn't enough; the driver took us to the police station. Eventually we arrived there half an hour late. Charming couple and very friendly. Packed the kids off to bed and found much to our surprise that we were being taken out to dinner without the children to Fosters Steak House* [still running]. *Lovely meal. Collected the kids and they took us back to the Majestic.*

### Day 62 (Saturday 31st December) – New Year's Eve with Betty and Alfred

**Julian:** *Betty rang first thing in morning. Invited us to come and stay for a few days. We had intended to go to Sentosa on Monday and either rent a chalet or camp. Little did Betty or us know we would be staying for over a week. Mad rush to get packed up. I went out with the kids intending to go down to Jardine Steps* [today's HarbourFront] *to find out about camping but time was running out. We went to the photographic shop but no film ready yet. Betty was late picking us up and we waited for ¾ of an hour outside after vacating our rooms.*

*Hotel was S $102 which was quite reasonable for three days. Had a good lunch and a rest in the afternoon.*

*View from our ride in the Sentosa cable car in January 2024*

*I woke up feeling really foul with the runs and belly cramp. Heaven knows what it was. We dragged up to Katong with Michelle and bought a Kodak Instamatic for James and a whistling train for Peter. Also trousers for the boys which turned out to be far too big. After laying down and being dosed up with pills by Alfred I forced myself down to dinner. Betty was doing a special dinner for New Year's Eve and had some friends in, Pat and wife from next door. It was good and I was glad I hadn't missed out. We all felt too tired to see the New Year in and I think it was only next morning early that Father Christmas came with a camera for James, a Six Million Dollar Man for Mark and a whistling train for Peter.*

## Day 63 (Sunday 1st January 1978) – A sickly New Year

**Julian:** *New Years' Day. I had the 'runs' which increased alarmingly throughout the day. The Lees went to church apart from Alfred; said he was a Heathen. Siesta after lunch followed by a walk around the Botanic Gardens [close to where Jess and I now live] as darkness was falling. Then went to food stalls just outside and tried soya bean milk. I felt terrible, Peter had liquid diarrhoea and*

*Audrey vomited copiously all over the place. What a group. Happy New Year!!*
*By the way, the kids loved their presents.*

## Chapter Ten

# Singapore

*Monday 2nd – Sunday 8th January 1978*

Well, no diary entries this week until Saturday 7th January. We must have been sick all week – thank God for Betty and Alfred's generosity in letting us stay with them in their Mountbatten Road home. However, we did manage to visit Haw Par Villa (otherwise known as 'Tiger Balm Gardens'), from where, as I write, Jess and I have just returned, and which is worthy of further mention... Built in the 1930's by Burmese-Chinese brothers Aw Boon Haw ('tiger') and Aw Boon Par ('leopard') of Tiger Balm fame, the gardens were declared public property and turned into a park after their deaths. The park contains over 1,000 statues and 150 giant dioramas depicting scenes from Chinese mythology, folklore, legends, history, and illustrations of various aspects of Confucianism. During the 1970s and 1980s, the park was a major local attraction welcoming at least a million visitors a year.

*I would like to have met the Haw Par brothers!*

One of Singapore's best-selling authors and resident since 1996, Dagenham's own Neil Humphreys, describes Tiger Balm Gardens perfectly in his 2015 book Saving a Sexier Island following a 10-year return visit:

> Certainly, the setting had already changed. I arrived at an MRT station, via an MRT line, that didn't exist a decade ago. As I marched purposefully up the villa's slope at its entrance, I sincerely hope that nothing else had changed… For its own sake Haw Par Villa still had to be terrible, macabre, distasteful and offensive…

> Luckily it was. It really was….

> Strolling around the decaying theme park, which was near deserted despite the free admission, the old favourites remained. In the broad thriftiness and virtues tableau, children were encouraged to respect the value of hard work and law and order by admiring a thief getting his teeth pulled out, a policeman punching a gangster repeatedly in his bloodied, pulpy forehead and a loan shark settling an unpaid debt in an unorthodox fashion...

> Thankfully, the iconic Ten Courts of Hell remained open. There cannot be many Singaporeans over the age of say, 30, who do not have a vivid memory of visiting the Ten Courts of Hell. The tableau of hellish retribution isn't easily forgotten…

> Inside the darkened, ghoulish exhibition of eternal punishment in the afterlife, the images of burning bodies and decapitated heads

were only marginally less affecting than watching a Chinese mother provide commentary for her two wide-eyed young children. At the Seventh Court of Hell, she pointed at the hideous sculpture and said: 'Ah, read that one ah... Rumour mongers... People who make up stories get their tongues pulled out. You see? Mustn't make up stories one.' At the Sixth Court of Hell, however, guilty folks were being sawn into two for the heinous crime of misusing books. I'm all for that.

And I'm all for Haw Par Villa. Universal Studios and the gardens at Marina Bay have their place, but they're distinctly un-Singaporean in their appeal...

But Haw Par Villa is as Singaporean as Singlish. Incomprehensible to some and just plain daft to others, Haw Par Villa is viewed with a degree of confusion and bemusement by outsiders but instantly recognised and understood by almost every Singaporean. Every country has a theme park of some description. Only Singapore has Haw Par Villa. It's silly, inefficient, old-fashioned, weird and makes no money. It's the anti-tourist attraction in a modern economy, entirely anathema to New Singapore. The macabre oddity practically raises a middle finger to town planners and number crunchers. And it will always have more of a Singaporean soul than an American theme park designed in United States and financed by a Malaysian casino operator.[1]

I couldn't agree more with Neil. Having read his really good book (amongst many others by him on Singapore) a few months ago, I was convinced that the place must have shut down by now. An early morning bike ride, just a few weeks ago, proved me wrong. After recognising it from our trip photos, and nearly falling off my bike, I resolved to re-visit and take some present-day pics for my book. It took a while but there was

---

1 Neil Humphreys, *Saving a Sexier Island: Notes from Old Singapore*, Marshal Cavendish International (Asia) Pte Ltd, 2015.

something immensely satisfying about finding Confucius and the Tale of Madam White Snake again after half a lifetime.

*The tales to accompany the statues at Tiger Balm Gardens*

*Haw Par Villa (Tiger Balm Gardens) – then and now, with Betty and Audrey Lee either side of Confucious, top left*

**Day 69 (Saturday 7th January) – The Docks**

**Julian:** *Collected van today. Becky did a huge shop in the morning while I looked after all the kids. She was doing leg of lamb tonight. About 12:00 o'clock I set off in a taxi with James, Mark and Audrey. Taxi driver dropped us at the wrong gate. Then had to walk back to pass office to get a pass. James found an identity card which we dropped in at police station next door. Then another taxi to gate four and a long walk down the Wharf to Godown 18. Various forms to be filled in and a walk back to Godown 15/16 to pay wharf fees (28 S$). Van had obviously been entered but nothing as far as I could tell been stolen. We had in fact acquired an extra torch. The hatchways to air cleaner and gas had been removed? Customs. No real damage. After sorting out car and reconnecting battery was soon out of the docks. No hassles at customs. Fairly straight forward drive back to 777* [Mountbatten Road]. *Kids decided to unpack car. Beautiful dinner of leg of lamb, roast potatoes, etc but kids were tired and naughty.*

I have a vague recollection of being very excited that we finally had our 'home' back and all our things within it, such as Lego. I imagine that I led the unpacking of the van with great enthusiasm!

**Day 70 (Sunday 8th January) – Running Repairs**

**Julian:** *Morning spent trying to sort car out with kids help. Seat near the side door had been broken yet again the day before* [probably by me 'sorting out' the van] *and needed sticking. In the afternoon we went over to the Booth's hotel and admired all their new buys. Jamie vomited all over their bed and looked really peaky. Luckily, he perked up and we were able to leave the kids with Betty and go to dinner with Phillip and Annette. They lived in a posh flat and unfortunately the evening was quite a strain. We never did seem to mix.*

My parents were egalitarians – Mum grew up in a working-class home in Crayford and while Dad is definitely on the 'posh' side, 8 years of being married to Mum and 4 ½ years living in Australia had scrubbed away any snobby attitudes he may have been exposed to in the Surrey village where he grew up. I can understand how it would have been tricky to relate to others who didn't share the same kind of open-minded views that they had. Mind you, I think almost anyone would be left scratching their head at their wacky plan to drive halfway round the world with 7 people in a camper van, four of them age 7 down to 6 months old!

Chapter Eleven

# Singapore Preparations

*Monday 9th – Friday 13th January 1978*

Another week of final frantic preparations, purchases, repairs and a last bit of sightseeing. Eight passport pictures for six of us for visas, filling our Gaz bottles, medicine, letters and an ultra-modern but eye wateringly expensive Sony radio cassette. Andrew was unwell, which delayed our departure, but did mean that we got to see *James Bond, The Spy Who Loved Me* at the cinema. Every cloud …

### Day 71 (Monday 9th January) – Gas, Marty Feldman and Peter Chews

**Julian:** *After breakfast, left with James* [the Lee's driver] *to look for photo booth. Found one in Orchard Road. Also took all of our film in for developing. Eight pictures of six of us took some time to complete and quite a number of 50c pieces. Later I went back to town with Peter. Camping shop did not refill cylinders. Dragged up to Orchard Road in a rickshaw and eventually found the dealer. That way it would take a week. Taxi to Beach Road and eventually found the people who did it. That even would take 24 hours. Anyway, I was able to get rid of the cylinders. Taxi back to Clifford Pier to arrange the car insurance. Then picked up the Vanquin syrup and letters at PO. Two from Lynn and PC from Dianne. Rickshaw to meet the others who had been to see Marty Feldman. Back home. Dianne had phoned and phoned again at 4:00 PM. James took us to meet her at 7th Storey Hotel and then we all went on to Peter*

*Chews and bought a $456 Sony radio cassette and two Seiko watches* [$1 SGD was worth around 23p in 1977]. *Got a few free beers for our efforts. Took ages to find a taxi back home. Lovely pork and roast potatoes for dinner.*

## Day 72 (Tuesday 10th January) – Jurong

**Julian:** *A very wet day. Spent morning fixing the seat and car fan we recently bought. In afternoon went off to Jurong. Too wet to see the bird park so we spent most of the afternoon looking around the Science Complex. Kids loved it pressing buttons and watching chickens hatch. Then a trip up Jurong hill and tower. Back to town to buy a couple of calculators for $22.80 each before collecting Audrey. An evening of eating drinking and talking.*

The Singapore Science Centre had only opened a month before we visited, more than two decades after it was first conceived. Its massive cost (in 1977) of S$20 million demonstrated just how serious the Singapore government was about promoting interest and learning in science and technology amongst its citizens. Singapore was industrialising rapidly and as such a tiny nation with no natural resources, education was key to its success. I'm not sure whether this is what did it, but as my friends and family will bear witness to, I have had a lifelong obsession with chicken impersonations!

## Day 73 (Wednesday 11th January) – Andy unwell

**Julian:** *What a day!! We had gone to bed late the night before and Andrew had been really difficult so we were feeling rather ******. Andrew's rash was worse than ever and he still had diarrhoea. Beck and Betty took him along to Alfred's clinic...*

**Becky:** *where he decided that with a temperature and diarrhoea to put him on antibiotics plus slight sedative. I spent most of the day holding him. Betty took us out shopping in the afternoon to the Arts and Crafts centre. Tried to buy Betty a present but she was far too nosy. We did buy 4 kites and mini furniture for Audrey and to send home. Finally, we dragged home about 6:30 PM tired, exhausted, and still with grotty baby.*

## Day 74 (Thursday 12th January) – Packing

**Becky:** *Spent all day packing or rather all morning holding Andrew, he was dreadful, and finally packed a bit. Dianne came late morning had lunch at Betty's. I went supermarket shopping. We packed until late that night. Andrew terrible again. Finally went to bed thinking about staying another day. Andrew was grotty and we wanted to get him better. Also, terrible nappy rash.*

Julian: *In morning I had gone to AA taking Peter with me to get export order and bill of lading. Then went to Handicraft Centre and bought Betty a vase and some brandy for Alfred. Then took taxi to Health Centre. Would not sign without an extra certificate. Then off to People's Park Complex to look for bag for Audrey. No luck. Got some money changed to Malaysian.*

## Day 75 (Friday 13th January) – The Spy Who Loved Me

**Julian:** *Decided to stay yet another day so we could rest. Had dashed into town at 7:00 AM, when James took Michelle to school, to sort out Andrew's smallpox certificate. Had to wait till 8:30 before office opened. Medical officer very reluctant to stamp because Alfred had only signed in one place. Taxi back home. Phoned Dianne but she had left hotel. Phoned Mr. Lee who told us we only needed to change dates on the forms. Luckily Dianne phoned immediately after and came round half an hour later. Sorted things during morning. In afternoon went to see James Bond, 'The Spy Who Loved Me'. Very exciting. Great rush afterwards to get the parcels packed and posted to England. Also went in camper to buy petrol and playpen. After a superb dinner more packing of camper and sorting out. Attempted to go to bed at reasonable hour but Andrew got in a real paddy which lasted over one hour.*

# PART III
# MALAYSIA & THAILAND
## *(1024 miles)*

~

*Malaysia: Our route from 777 Mountbatten Road to Batu Ferringhi.*

Map © 2025 Google

Chapter Twelve

# Malaysia

*Saturday 14th – Sunday 22nd January 1978*

Finally, after 2½ weeks in Singapore, (which was not supposed to have been more than a week), we set off up the Malay peninsula. Despite illness and administrative headaches, we had had a wonderful stay, not least due to the generous hospitality of Betty and Alfred. From here on, we were on our own; well, plus Dianne until we reached Nepal. Her diary entries add welcome flavour and, until this point, a much absent female perspective, with Mum somewhat pre-occupied by baby, toddler and let's face it, as responsible and grown up as we were, 6 and 7 year old boys.

During our first week in Malaysia, we head up the west coast through the rubber plantations to camp near the old Portuguese port town of Malacca. After a futher night on the west coast, much to the locals' curiosity, we head into Kuala Lumpar for administrative tasks, to meet up with the Booths, and for van repairs. We cross the Malay peninsula to the east coast via the Batu Caves, meeting many more curious, friendly and helpful locals wherever we camped. The diary does a good job of telling the story.

### Day 76 (Saturday 14th January) – Off to Malaysia

Julian: *A reasonable night's sleep. Beck was up bright and early. I wasn't feeling in a very efficient mood. Eventually got everything squeezed into camper and left about 10 after photographs all round. Unfortunately, Alfred had already gone off to work. Beck had managed to buy a second bucket.*

*Farewell to the Lees at Mountbatten Road*

*After getting lost in the one-way system we eventually got out of the city on the correct road. Changed some Singapore dollars at a bank and spent the rest of the change on petrol. Not too much hassle at the border. Did not stop at JB [Johor Bahru]. Slow drive getting stuck behind numerous lorries. Frequent heavy showers. Malaysian drivers have a habit of overtaking and cutting in sharply in front of you. Saw a nasty accident between a motorbike and lorry with two bodies lying in the road at awkward angles. Many people around so we didn't get involved. Pushed on to Malacca where we camped on Long Beach. Quite a pleasant evening apart from Peter's tantrums. Nude swim in the sea.*

**Dianne:** *Finally left at 10.30 am. Got to border and very easy to get through which was good. Malaysia is so empty after Singapore. Green fields also lots of rubber plantations. Trees look smaller than a gum tree but all have taps and small buckets collecting latex – rather interesting. Passed motorbike accident just outside Batur Pahat. Horrible. One for sure had a broken pelvis. Reached Malacca which is a lovely old town with canal passing through it – also old*

98

*sailing ship just off the shore. Hong Kong looking one with white sales. Finally decided to camp by a volleyball court near the sea – very pleasant. Went for night skinny dip – no sure how clean the water was but too dark to see and very pleasant. Early to bed.*

Malaysia was once the world's largest producer of rubber, the history of which has close connections to Singapore's Botanic Gardens, a UNESCO World Heritage Site, near our present-day home. Established in 1859, the beautiful 82-hectare Gardens played an important role in fostering agricultural development in Singapore and the region. One of the earliest and most important successes was the introduction, experimentation, and promotion of Para Rubber, Hevea brasiliensis, due largely to the Gardens' first Director, Henry Nicholas Ridley. 'Mad Ridley' or 'Rubber Ridley' as he was known, published over 500 books, described over 4,000 new plant species and pioneered Malaya's rubber industry. He researched the commercial potential of rubber, including the various methods to tap the tree's latex without causing permanent harm to the tree, (as described in Dianne's diary entry), and preparing the latex for sale. As a result, rubber become the region's major cash crop when the existing coffee plantations were destroyed by disease. By 1920, Malaya was producing over half the world's rubber, and rubber is still an important crop in the region today, though in Malaysia, rubber plantations have largely been replaced by palm. The oil is more profitable than natural rubber, which is gradually being displaced by synthetic rubber.

The horrific motorbike accident scene has stuck with me; seeing body parts in the road made quite an impression on a 7-year-old boy. I recall a Land Rover ambulance with a Red Cross on the side and the para medics throwing the riders' limbs into the back of the vehicle. Dad thinks my young, over-imaginative mind may have slightly embellished this, which Dianne's 'broken pelvis' also hints at. (Young minds can get quite creative can't they!) Dad's understated *'so we didn't get involved'* hints at his tendency, following medical training, to know when help is useful, and help whenever possible. He turned one BA flight from the US around, mid Atlantic, for a lifesaving landing in Newfoundland. Dad tells the story:

"A Scottish Guy developed a Pulmonary Embolism (clot in the lung) which can be fatal unless treated rapidly. This guy was pretty sick and had to be evacuated asap, but we were a third of the way across the Atlantic by this time, the nearest landfall being Newfoundland. We did what we could for him and I eventually convinced the pilot that we had to turn back. I think if we hadn't, he would not have survived. So, we got him evacuated into medical care at St John's, Newfoundland. Long delays after that; the airport wasn't used to dealing with planes as large as the 747 so they got the balance of the refuelling all wrong which then had to be readjusted. Then we had to have our wings de-iced and all the time the weather was deteriorating with a snowstorm coming in. We did eventually manage to take off in the middle of this snowstorm and resume our journey in luxury, as we were upped to First Class and treated to numerous free drinks. I reckon well deserved as I had already treated one other medical emergency on that trip. Got back to Heathrow about 9 hours late."

### Day 77 (Sunday 15th January) – Aliens have landed

**Becky:** *Eventually got away about 12:00 o'clock. Caused much local entertainment, many people in little huddles.*

**Julian:** *Took picture of them staring at the camp. At port Dickson stopped for lunch and had a swim on the beach. Then onto KL [Kuala Lumpur]. Somehow managed to bypass the city altogether and landed up in some suburban estate. Asked at a garage where we could camp and they pointed the way to Morib. At another garage we gathered this was 30 miles outside KL and the only place to camp. On the way out there we found it was halfway back to port Dickson.*

*Anyway we comforted ourselves in the fact that we should be camping at a proper site, or so we thought. But where was this site at Morib? We travelled up and down asking people who pointed this way and that. Eventually we stopped at a house to fill our water bottles and were asked in for tea and biscuits. The chap who worked in the Dunlop factory in KL then led us to a bit of spare ground on the beach next to the guest house. No campsite. He then proceeded to help us set up camp and hung around for ages peering at this and that.*

*Curious onlookers at Long Beach, Malacca; Campsite at Morib, and our generous helper*

**Dianne:** *Left about midday – drove through lots of rubber plantations and palm tree plantations – they make oil from the palm trees. Stopped at Port Dickson for lunch – seaside resort – very nice swim. Then headed for KL – kept on the freeway and were through to KL very fast. Stopped at the garage to ask about campsite and after several directions headed for Morib which we discovered was ½ way back to Port Dickson. Then when we got to Morib there was only a beach and no actual campsite. Don't think there are any campsites in Malaysia. Finally stopped a boy to ask him where to go and he took us to his home where we got some water and they gave us tea and biscuits – very friendly people. They showed us where we could camp. Campsite is near sea again – another midnight swim. Can see lights of fishing boats which are beautiful.*

This week we cross peninsular Malaysia to the east coast during the period of the Hindu Thaipusam religious festival, which falls on the full moon in the tenth month of Tamil Almanac. We encounter the celebrations, Vietnamese Boat People, intense and claustrophobic scrutiny by locals, a shipwreck and beautiful east coast sunsets. The diary does such a good job of telling the story ...

## Day 78 (Monday 16th January) – Kuala Lumpur

**Julian:** *Next morning our visitor was back at 08.45. We were feeling really efficient and managed to get away by 9am after filling up with water at the nearby Guest House. After running round the suburbs and asking at the nearby police station we found that the main road did in fact lead to the City Centre. Heaven knows where we had messed it up the evening before. Luckily we found a parking place and squeezed in. First stop a bank and the tourist office followed by drinks and chicken and rice. Then provisional enquiries at the shipping office. Everyone was feeling hot and 'crotchety' so we decided to leave it at that. Dianne and I changed money and I went back to the tourist office. Luckily I did for we found the AA had changed its address. We eventually drove to the hotel where the AA was situated and got the address where the Booths were staying.*

*For the next two hours we went back and forth looking for this place. Eventually we picked up a girl waiting at a bus stop who knew where it was and after passing through some pretty heavy rain and floods, we joined up with the Booths. Their host took us out and we found a cheap Chinese Hotel where we stayed the night, a large room with four beds. Bought a variety of dishes from the stalls outside and ate in our room.*

**Dianne:** *Off to a good start – up at 7 am – swim in the sea watching fishing boats come in. Then left 9 AM for KL – after getting lost 10 times finally got into city centre – did banking, ship and tourist office. Then got lost about 3 times again before finding the Booths. So nice to see them in the end – they are going straight to Penang where we will meet them. People are so good here – the only reason we found them was a girl at the bus stop came with us to direct us. Decided to stay in hotel at night in KL so we can pick up tickets in AM, finish all jobs and leave for countryside.*

## Day 79 (Tuesday 17th January) – Mum's wobble

**Julian:** *Dianne went off to town early. Becky had a 'down' and phoned up travel agents to find the cost of flying home only to depress herself more. I eventually* *got off to town with James, Mark and Peter and went to the shipping agents to buy the tickets. Beck was in a better mood when I got back having listened to the radio all morning. We got to packing and were off an hour later. Found our way back to the Booths to tell them our latest plans. Eventually got off and drove back into town and out on the North Road. Reached Templer Park where we camped. It was quite beautiful tropical jungle with some beautiful butterflies, but the rubbish, heat and mosquitoes put us off somewhat. Rained during the night and we found that we had some drying out to do the next morning.*

**Dianne:** *Up early and went sightseeing in KL – took pictures of train station which is a huge white monstrosity with turrets everywhere and barn swallows by the thousands. Then went to Nat Mosque which is a $10 million structure built around 10 years ago – huge empty tiled building and had to wear black robes and scarf. To travel agent to get boat tickets then went to museum – good with lots of Malay history past and present. Goodbye to Booths then onto Templer Nat Park – lovely walk through rainforest and swim in stream which was relaxing.*

*Kuala Lumpur Railway Station – famous for its mixture of Eastern and Western Architecture*

103

### Day 80 (Wednesday 18th January) – Batu Caves

**Julian:** *Off to a late start. A few repairs on the car including the accelerator which had been sticking for the last few days. Drove back a few miles to the Batu Caves where we had refreshments and climbed the 300 steps to the main cave. Nothing very impressive apart from its size. They were preparing for the festival and the other caves were unfortunately closed. Then on to the East Coast Road and a long monotonous drive to Kuantan where we set up camp on the beach in the gathering dusk.*

**Dianne:** *Up early but lots of fiddling about after everything got wet in rain during the night. Car needs fixing and general mishmash. Finally got to Batu caves – climbed all 260 steps to top which was just a large cave – not even a spectacular view really – only thing really impressive was the staircase with archways with colourful figures on Hindu temple. After drove to Kuantan on the east coast and camped on a beach. Drive through mostly wood rainforest area – lots of timber trucks. Midnight swim. Water lovely & warm.*

*Reed shop on way over to the East Coast*

*Batu Caves 18th Jan 1978 – 300 steps up; Pete and Dianne*

*Constant onlookers at Kuantan campsite*

## Day 81 (Thursday 19th January) – Mixing with the locals

**Julian:** *A quiet day relaxing on the beach. Constant inspection by the locals. Very interested in us. I did some more tent reproofing but even with three more tins failed to finish. We had a lot of fun splashing about with the canoe. In the evening we lit a fire and got some locals to go and buy us some beer which we shared with them. Late to bed again.*

**Dianne:** *Relaxing day by beach – general wash and clean up. In & out of water all day. Sea isn't very blue but lovely temperature. Clean beach. Boats just offshore fishing and what looks like an oil derrick in distance. Unfortunately, the beach is rather near the village and road so lots of cars, trucks and observers.*

### Day 82 (Friday 20th January) – Pied Pipers

**Julian:** *Late up so we didn't leave till 10:30. Some quite nice scenery up the East Coast but the beaches weren't as fabulous as we had been led to believe. Perhaps we had been spoilt by the Australian beaches. The problem was getting down to them. We tried several dead ends. Had a grotty lunch in a grotty cafe in Dungun then had to stop to mend the rear door which refused to close. For ages we looked for a campsite. There were either palm trees with masses of houses or no shade. Eventually found a rather nice spot in amongst the palm trees outside Kuala Terengganu with only a few houses around. Set up camp with 40 plus people, mainly children, looking on. Throughout the evening we had smiling faces peering in at the windows or staring in through the doors from the darkness outside and listening to our radio cassette.*

**Dianne:** *(127 miles) Left campsite about 10 am and stopped at basket workshop where they had some lovely things. Countryside is rainforest and mangroves with glimpses of palm lined beaches. At the workshop the owner gave us some delicious coconut. Finally stopped at one of those palm lined beaches near Kuala Terengganu and had about 40 beautiful children watching us put up the tent – others on the beach flying kites they made themselves – large bird one.*

### Day 83 (Saturday 21st January) – East Coast beach fun

**Julian:** *A day on the beach. Crowds all day staring at us. Quite windy and the waves pounded in. Shampooed and aired the car carpet but did not make much impression. Had quite a bit of fun mucking around in the canoe. Kids got on quite well with the locals and played totem tennis with them. The night before we had had nude swims. Tonight I went to bed early but the girls went in for a dip.*

**Dianne:** *Very lazy day – swimming, reading, sleeping. Beautiful just to watch the surf which is really quite high and rough. Sometimes its difficult to concentrate on the sea because there are so many locals standing in front of you watching you. Interesting place though with men fishing from the shore this morning with nets. Behind us is a wooden house with goats and cows wandering around.*

### Day 84 (Sunday 22nd January) – Sightseeing and new helpers

**Julian:** *In spite of good intentions it was 7.30 before we got up. Even so we were off by 10:00 AM. Went backwards a few miles to look at handicrafts and kites but didn't buy anything. Then onwards to Kuala Terengganu where we bought fresh bread and vegetables at the market. Got lost finding our way out of town. Lunch in a rain shelter of fresh bread, cheese, cucumber, banana and pineapple. Later we made a detour to Kampung Kuala Besut which was quite a charming fishing village with great character. Did some more food shopping, got some batik material and had lime drinks all round. Inquired about hiring a fishing boat to the island of Pulau Perkantian but apparently few boats going out because of the full moon.*

*Typical Malaysian home near Kuala Terengganu*

*Decorated Malaysian lorry*

*Getting late so we started to look for a camping spot. Followed a track for miles hoping to find a beach but no luck. Eventually found a flat piece of grass by a*

107

*communal rain hut and set up camp with the usual mass of faces looking on. At least we got them to help blow up the air beds.*

*Locals helping us to set up camp near Kuala Besut*

**Dianne:** *Left the campsite at 10 am with goodbyes from all the local children. Did a quick tour of kite and basket workshops – kites are beautiful made of batik in the shape of birds. Then quick tour of Kuala Terengganu which is rather filthy. Found a beautiful bread shop – sold bread steaming hot from the oven. Then headed for Kota Bahru. Made a slight detour to Kuala Besut which is a picturesque fishing village – all of the boats are in at present because it is a full moon and since they fish at night with lights they can't go out when there is a full moon. Went to the market. We camped in a village nearby amongst rice paddies and wooden houses and right beside an old meeting house. I am sure the locals have never seen anything like us before and soon had about 50 watching – nice friendly people – real country farming people.*

Chapter Thirteen

# East Coast to Penang

*Monday 23rd – Sunday 29th January 1978*

My brother Mark's contribution this week and his recommendation of the fantastic book, *Neverest*, by Maxim and Stefan Ivanov – a father and son team who built their own boat in their garage in Bulgaria and rowed it across the Atlantic in 2020 – have given me inspiration. Father and son each tell their incredible story in their own words on alternate days. Mark's recollection of 23rd January below gives a unique and vivid picture of the beach in Kota Bahru, of which I have no recollection. So too do Dianne's diary entries of the time she was travelling with us. It really illustrates how our trip meant so much to so many of us. This week we also encounter the Hindu Thaipusam religious festival, which falls on the full moon in the tenth month of Tamil Almanac, Vietnamese Boat People, intense and claustrophobic scrutiny by locals, a shipwreck and beautiful east coast sunsets.

### Day 85 (Monday 23rd January) – Refugees on the beach

**Julian:** *Packed up with 50 to 100 faces looking on. Got away at 9am and an uninteresting drive to Kota Bahru. Got lost in the town and eventually found the train station. Had ideas about putting the van on a train either back to Kuala Lipis in the Genting Highlands or to Yala in Thailand. Found however there was a road to Yala and decided to drive. Thought we would find the*

*'Beach of Passionate Love' before going back to town to shop. However, this was easier said than done.*

There really was a beach called the 'Beach of Passionate Love', or 'Pantai Cinta Berahi' in Malay. It is near Kota Bharu in the state of Kelantan, close to the Thai border. Originally called 'Pantai Semut Api', the 'beach of the fire ants', it is possible that the name was changed in the 1950's in an attempt to attract tourists. It certainly made Dad curious. However, Kelantan is a very religious state ruled by an Islamic government, where dancing, cinemas, craven images and the consumption of alcohol are frowned upon. Not surprising then that this suggestive name, the 'Beach of Passionate Love', was unpopular locally and it was changed to 'Pantai Cahaya Bulan' – the 'beach of the clear moon'. Much more respectable.

*One of the many rivers complicating road access to the beach at Kota Bharu*

**Becky:** *We were all in a good mood at first but gradually as we drove up and down the coast looking for a camping place we got more and more fed up as we just couldn't get near the beach either because there was no track or a river between us and the sea. Eventually we plumped for a place just off the main track but near water …*

**Julian:** *… in the centre of village. The crowds soon gathered. Beck and I and the kids went off for a swim and to look at the wreck of a small freighter beached* *on the sand. The boys loved that especially as one could get on board. The name had been changed from Moon River to Success Star. They say changing the name of a ship is unlucky.*

*We also looked for another site. We found a beautiful place which could only be reached from the beach. How we wished we had a 4-wheel drive. When we returned the crowds had gathered in force. Dianne was really very upset. That evening we were continually bothered by dozens of peering faces coming closer and closer. We all got quite manic about it and kept shooing them away but they kept coming back. The children seemed to think it was a great game of 'cat and mouse'. We hated that place because of the people but really it was a lovely situation.*

**Dianne:** *Went straight to the train station to find out there was a road to Thailand so our decision is made. I was very glad to be going to Thailand. Decided to try and find a camping place before going marketing but headed across this dreadful road and by the time we got to the beach we didn't want to come back. It was a memorable night for me as it was the night that all the stares finally drove me mad. The Littles went off to the beach and I stayed at the tent and was continually hounded by people walking around the tent – knocking it, calling out and peering in every crevice – it felt like I was trapped. The crowds continued all night. It was such a shame because it was a lovely village with beautiful beach and lovely ladies fishing on the beach. Because it is close to border we woke up with about 6 army guys watching the bay for Vietcong.*

*Local women fishing on the beach near Kota Bharu*

**Mark:** *We helped set up the tent and then played on the beach. James and I were having fun on the beach but all these people were there, they were dressed poorly with lots of rips in their shirts and trousers. At first they were friendly with us and though they spoke a different language they smiled and laughed with us. Soon, many of them walked away up the beach. One man stayed with us. He was smoking a cigarette. The next thing I knew this man grabbed my left hand and would not let go. After a moment he took the cigarette from his mouth and pushed the burning end into the centre of my palm. As I screamed, I pulled so hard that my arm broke free. At which point I ran up the beach to the camp area and did not stop until I reached the van. I was sobbing as I tried to explain what had happened so I couldn't get my words out. I think James was completely unaware of what the man did as he gleefully played in the waves lapping the pure white sand a few metres away from where I had been laughing with the smoking man.*

*By the time I went back, James had already followed me up the beach and the man had disappeared into the far distance. It must have only been a split second where the hot ember of the burning cigarette touched my palm as the pain soon went away. I settled down into bed in the tent and Dad read James and I The Magic FarAway Tree by Enid Blighton. I love this book. I hope we leave this place tomorrow – I'm scared of the people in rags on the beach.*

This was a low point in our trip, which comes across vividly in the diary entries, even if we didn't know the context and the real reasons at the time. My brother just knew that a man who had been all smiles one minute had suddenly and inexplicably tortured him the next. I have no recollection of this, and it was only in his contribution to my research that I became aware of Mark's plight – what a horrible and frightening thing for a six-year-old to have experienced alone. I wanted to know why, and in my research, I found the period 1978-9 was the height of the Vietnamese refugee crisis that followed the end of the Vietnam War in 1975. Saigon (now Ho Chi Minh City) fell to the communist north Vietnamese forces, 10 years after the first US troops were sent in to support the more democratic south. The war had been a proxy for the Cold War, in which democracy, the south and the USA were on the losing side.

The fall of Saigon triggered waves of refugees, fleeing political oppression, poverty, and ongoing war. Many who had fought for the south, worked with the US, or held positions in the south Vietnamese government were sent to 're-education camps': political prisons where inmates were indoctrinated to the to the ideology of their new government. Torture was common. One million Vietnamese were sent to these camps; thousands tried to escape. Many refugees were Chinese ethnic minorities, fleeing Draconian new laws introduced in 1978 enabling the government to seize Chinese owned businesses. The Hoa people – Vietnamese citizens with Chinese ancestry – were particularly targeted and made up a large proportion of the Boat People.

Crossing the border was not an option. Vietnam was at war with Cambodia, which was supported by China, and Laos was ruled by communists similar to, and supported by, the Vietnamese government. So, the only escape was via the South China Sea, often in small, unseaworthy boats, giving rise to the name 'Boat People'. Where we camped at Kota Bahru was the closest landfall to the southernmost point of Vietnam from where many refugees departed. The number of boat people leaving Vietnam and arriving safely in other countries totalled almost 800,000 between 1975 and 1995. Facing danger from Thai pirates, over-crowded boats and storms, many died at sea – between 200,000 and 400,000 boat people according to the United Nations High Commission for Refugees. A huge number, horrific not only for its magnitude but also the haziness of the true death toll.

We had arrived at the height of this refugee crisis, when the greatest numbers of Boat People were arriving. Nowadays of course, with the internet, smart phones and a voracious global media, we would probably have chosen to avoid the area. But we didn't know – even afterwards, so it seems from the diary. In hindsight it is all too clear why these poor, tormented 'people in rags on the beach' would not leave us alone, why there was such a heavy military presence and why the atmosphere was so different to the usual friendly welcome we experienced from locals. It may also explain Mark's cigarette burn – did the sight of blonde Caucasians on the beach lead this man to think we were American? Did he blame the USA for the atrocities of the war and their plight, and was this some twisted form of revenge? Dianne agrees in her Facebook comments on my weekly blog post:

> *Agree with diaries above that Kota Bahru was a low point. Looking back of course I think your comments are right that many of the beach residents were likely refugees from Vietnam and in desperate conditions there living on the beach. I remember clearly the cigarette incident with Mark and, while not in my diary either, it was as described by Mark. My recollection is also that Becky went out on the beach into the crowd and was very angry asking how they could do that to a little boy.*

### Day 87 (Tuesday 24th January) – Some peace in Thailand

**Julian:** *Went back to Kota Bharu. Did some shopping in the market. Even there, masses of people crowded around the van. Jamie bought a penknife and Becky got upset with the crowds. Then off to Thai border and at Pasir Mas had sandwiches just before the border. Much filling out of forms and stamping both on the Malaysian and Thailand side of the river. Luckily, we did not need visas for a short stay. Travelled back to the coast where a friendly policeman helped us to buy beer in Tak Bai. Then on towards Narathiwat. Found a small track leading down to the beach. Really deserted compared to our previous campsite. Sat on the beach and drank beer waiting to see if the hordes came. Only three or four appeared and they kept their distance. Went to bed in a peaceful frame of mind. In fact, after a whole day's drive, we found that we were only about 15 miles up the coast from where we were before.*

**Dianne:** *Left fairly early and nice to be leaving. Went into Kota Bahru shopping in a fantastic market and bought some batik. Then we headed for Thailand – on the way passing a small Thai Pusa celebration at Tumpat. A few men in a trance had pins through their tongues. This celebration also takes place on the same day at the Batu Caves in KL – much bigger, but same actions of* *participants.*

*Usual border formalities but no problems. Roads are really good here. Decided to drive up the coast. Found a fantastic campsite – lonely stretch of beach with no people and we sat on the beach and drank beer to celebrate. Then had a relaxing night just sitting outside under a full moon by the sea – this is what it should be like!*

'Thaipusam' is a temple festival celebrated by Hindus of Tamil descent (their most important public rite) between January 14 and February each year. The name is derived from Thai which means '10th', (being celebrated in the 10th month of Tamil Almanac), and *pusam* meaning 'when the moon is at its brightest'. In 'Thai' 1978 the full moon fell on Tuesday 24th January and so too it turned out, did it on the day I write this – 5th February 2023. Last night we were in downtown Singapore with my father-in-law who was visiting from England, and the Thaipusam festivities were being prepared. Our taxi driver told us that these typically involve a procession, followed by young men walking over hot coals, leading me to make the connection with our story and the photo below.

*Dancers, with cheeks pierced with spears, in a trance during a
Hindu religious festival*

Dedicated to Lord Subramaniam, (also known as Lord Murugan), a major South Indian god, the deity of youth, power and virtue, this festival is a time for repentance. This involves conditioning the body and mind for about a week before the festival by extensive prayer and fasting, before performing acts of penance or thanksgiving like carrying a 'kavadi' – a short wooden pole surmounted by a wooden arch, decorated with peacock feathers (symbolic of Murugan). Often, sharp skewers are pierced through the tongues, cheeks and bodies of kavadi-bearers as a practice of self-mortification. Why do this? According to the legend, devas or celestial beings at one time were so plagued by asura, or demons, that they pleaded with Lord Siva, to help them. Touched by their pleas, Lord Siva sent his son Subramaniam to conquer the asuras. After his victory Subramaniam appeared before his devotees bedecked with brilliant jewels, armed with a golden spear and seated on a chariot.

Thus, on Thaipusam day, Lord Subramaniam's image, adorned and decorated, is placed on a silver chariot before his devotees, which is then taken in a procession. As well as being acknowledged as a symbol of bravery, power, virtue, and beauty, Hindus believe that Lord Subramaniam is also the universal dispenser of favours. Hence, some who have made vows and pledges to Lord Subramaniam prove their gratitude to him by undergoing self-mortification on Thaipusam day. Not for me thanks!

*Narathiwat Beach – a lovely quiet camping site*

116

We only spent one full day and two nights in Thailand and just have the one picture above of our camp at Narathiwat Beach, but it sounds as though the peace and solitude after our harrowing experience the day before, was a welcome relief. Dad explains that we spent very little time in Thailand as we realised there was no point going further, not being able to get through the Burmese border (now Myanmar). I had always imagined that we drove to the border and were turned back. Apparently today there is a good highway through Myanmar; something which I am bearing in mind for my planned repeat of our trip 50 years on, in 2027.

### Day 88 (Wednesday 25th January) – Lazy day on Narathiwat Beach

**Julian:** *A nice lazy day on the beach. A few curious faces but nothing compared to the day before. Finished letter to the parents. Beck did lots of washing and I made several trips to collect water from a well at a ramshackle hut where an old woman with her five kids lived. We had an open fire in the evening and finished the beer.*

**Dianne:** *Spent relaxing day on the beach and a few people came. Very different than in Malaysia as they are quiet and shy and also look very poor and the children thin and have many sores. The beach is lovely but water very rough so not good for swimming. It is a fishing community and every night the whole village turns out to get the boats in. Sat by the campfire again at night and enjoyed the surf and the moon.*

### Day 89 (Thursday 26th January) – Back to Malaysia and 'beautiful orange'

**Julian:** *Got off to a reasonable start and headed for Narathiwat where we bought a small loaf of bread with the remaining few Baht's we had. Then on towards the Yala road. Good smooth roads and we drove fast only to find the engine was overheating. Topped up with water with little difference. After getting lost we eventually found the Yala road which was bumpy and winding. Stopped on the verge among the ants for lunch. Beck drove after that and I got sick reading to the kids and being bounced around in the back. A bit of a* *hassle at the customs at Batong what with form filling at the Thailand side and getting the Carnet exit stamp. Had to rush to the Malaysian side before 5:00 PM* [presumably the border closed then] *and got through fairly quickly, even with the customs officer asking me all about his bronchitis. Eventually put up in a guest house in Baling. Good night's sleep and beautiful orange* [Dad isn't sure what he was referring to! Perhaps the fruit, or a sunset ...].

**Dianne:** *Left our perfect spot early. Drove along the fantastic Thailand roads which are so smooth after Malaysia. Really a fun drive. I really like the Thai people. Fantastic lorries here – look like circus trucks and are decorated at the front and the sides. Scenery through the mountains was lush green with a river and gorges always in view. Border crossing again the usual. Stayed in a rest house in Baling and had a lovely shower and dinner out.*

## Day 90 (Friday 27th January) – Batu Ferrengi, Penang

**Julian:** *After our own breakfast set off for Penang. Not far to Butterworth. Plenty of evidence of Europeans and Australians with an RAAF base. Bit of a wait for the ferry but they seemed fairly well organised. A ride through Georgetown with the usual wrong turn and out on the North Coast Road to Batu Ferrengi. Just as we were wondering whether to turn back to see if a message had been left at the AA by the Booths, we saw their Land Rover parked on an open space next to the sea. Unfortunately, one of the buckets had been crushed and spilt by the water container so the afternoon was taken up with taking the carpet out and scrubbing it. Masses of things soaked including Dianne's quilt. Girls went down to the local shops with Denise.*

**Dianne:** *Short drive to Butterworth which is smoggy congested city. Then a super organised ferry trip to Penang which is much like Bali except even more Australians – permanent ones with the air force. Found the Booths and a campsite and a lovely beach in Batu Ferrengi. Water is lovely here – calm and warm and no seaweed and clean.*

Dad mentions the RAAF (Royal Australian Air Force) base in Butterworth. The base, still operational, is now run by the RMAF (Royal

Malaysian Air Force) and is the HQ for an Integrated Air (now re-designated 'Area') Defence System (IADS) for Peninsular Malaysia and Singapore, established under the 'Five Power Defence Arrangements' (FPDA). These are a series of multi-lateral agreements, signed in 1971, between Australia, Malaysia, New Zealand, Singapore, and the United Kingdom – all Commonwealth members that were once part of the British Empire. The FDPA resulted from the UK's decision to withdraw its armed forces east of Suez in 1967. Their 50th anniversary was celebrated in 2021, with joint air and naval displays involving the ships and aircraft of the member countries. Under the agreement the members are to consult each other 'immediately' in the event of threat or an armed attack for the purpose of deciding what measures to take, jointly or separately in response.

For us, passing through Butterworth in 1977 to catch the Penang ferry, it meant that unusually we weren't the only white faces in sight and were therefore not such a curiosity to the locals. Quite a relief, I imagine, for our parents and Dianne after our experience at Kota Bharu; bit of a come down for us kids though – no more games of 'cat and mouse'...

### Day 91 (Saturday 28th January) – Forms and travel stories

**Julian:** *Went into Georgetown by bus with Dianne and Mike. Filled out six yellow forms and then went back to the National Bank and after waiting an hour got an export stamp. On way back inquired about VW for Lynn. Caught bus back to Batu Ferrengi. A lazy afternoon swimming and relaxing. Met Nigel and Stella in their Ford estate van that night, who had just come back from KL. Sat talking and drinking coffee till late.*

**Dianne:** *Early start into Georgetown – very fascinating Chinese town. Very hot though. Had dinner at a stall but not very good. Had a swim then went shopping nearby. In the evening, Nigel and Stella a couple from England, arrived at the campsite. They have done the overland trip from London so had lots of very funny stories about their experiences.* [I'd love to hear some of those stories Nigel and Stella, if you're reading this!]

*Overlanders at Batu Ferrenhi campsite, including Nigel and Stella's Ford estate van and our Toyota Hiace with tent attached on right*

**Day 92 (Sunday 29th January) – Horns, fish & chips**

**Julian:** *A quiet day not doing much and tidying up, with a bit of swimming*

120

*here and there. I think I played around with the horns trying to get them to work again. Did get them going reluctantly every now and then. Went into the village in the evening for fish and chips.*

**Dianne:** *Relaxing day. Beach is lovely. Out in evening for fish and chips at local restaurant which was delicious.*

Chapter Fourteen

# Penang & the Chidambaram

*Mon 30th Jan – Sun 5th Feb 1978*

Thishis is the week we leave Southeast Asia for India aboard the *MV Chidambaram*. According to the diary, the ship had previously been with the French Line and was called the *Pasteur*. What was that you said about it being bad luck to change the name of a ship, Dad? A good part of this week is spent, (mainly by Dad), getting all the paperwork sorted for our voyage, but we still seemed to pack a fair bit in. Funiculars, snake temples, van maintenance, swimming and cruising…

**Day 93 (Monday 30th January) – Port authorities & more paperwork**

**Julian:** *One hell of a day. I spent all day in town with paperwork. I don't know what Beck did but I'm sure she had a hard day looking after four children. I went in with Denise and Mike in their Land Rover. First of all to Jamabuoys* [shipping agent] *to see if there were any tips. None, so I left the others and walked to the ferry to Butterworth. A long walk to the Customs House the other end. Masses of stamping and checking of all those horrible yellow forms and I had to fill in one extra. Downstairs I handed in a blue form and paid $10 what for I don't know. This all took ages then back to Jamabuoys. Arrived there 12:45. Their lunch was 1-2pm but the relevant person had already gone off and wouldn't be back till 2:30. So in a rage I went off to do some shopping.*

123

*Bought batteries, looked for zips, had noodle soup and a couple of beers. Found a bucket to be collected later and arrived back at Jamabuoys at 3pm only to find Mike still there and looking right 'pissed off'. One of his yellow forms with a receipt was missing and the Port Authorities would not accept the consignment. After paying them 950 $M I had to rush down to the Port Authorities before they closed at 4pm. Paid another $20 for 'handling charges' and the chap assured me everything was in order and nothing else to do. So dubiously I set off to the bus station collecting the bucket on the way and after a lot of waiting around got back to camp about 6:30 PM. Beck was still alive, and one side of the car had been cleaned by the boys.*

### Day 94 (Tuesday 31st January) – Jacobs Cream Crackers

**Julian:** *Another quiet day on the beach. Finished cleaning the car. First thing in morning went into town with Joseph* [another traveller] *and kids in our car. Took gas cylinders in to be filled. Joseph thought he knew where a new zip could be purchased and put into our tent, but they couldn't do it till after Chinese New Year. Filled up with petrol and got a huge tin of cream crackers and returned to camp. In afternoon fiddled with horns again and flushed out radiator. Every day at Batu Ferrengi had been lovely weather, the sea really warm. The luminescence of the water at night was incredible. I'm sure the boys loved it there. We blew up the canoe and an inner tyre tube.*

Dianne: *Quick trip to town to try and get zipper fixed but no luck. Then it was a clear up day back at the campsite.*

### Day 95 (Wednesday 1st February) – Funicular and Snake Temple

**Julian:** *A day of sightseeing. Got off about 10:30. Nigel and Stella were staying in camp, so they kept an eye on things while we were away. The Booths were also out for the day sorting out the remaining problems concerning the shipment of their Land Rover. We first went to see the Hindu temple with the third largest reclining Buddha in the world. Really ugly piece of statue but the temple was rather fascinating what with the ornate carvings and catacombs filled with vases of ashes. Then pushed off to the Funicular Railway. Rather clever* *engineering. Gradient 1:0.96 and two different systems. Really beautiful at the top of Penang Hill. Fantastic flowers. We splashed out on a meal at a local restaurant.*

**Dianne:** *Tour of the island. To reclining Buddha Temple first with an amazing statue of huge bold Buddha with extra long feet lying in the middle of the temple. Surrounding the Buddha are Chinese catacombs with ashes in urns in small wall recesses with picture of person on the front of the glass. Also various donation boxes. Next on the list was the funicular railway up Denang Hill – super steep. View from top was terrific with all of Penang and mainland Malaysia. Took about 1/2 hour to get up the hill changing cars ½ way up.*

The Penang Hill funicular railway was built in 1923 for the British colonial community to enjoy the cooler air of the Penang Hill. Dad's 'two systems' refers to two independent sections, (which operated until a 2010 upgrade), due to the difference in gradient between the lower and upper section. Passengers were required to change trains at the middle station. Each section had two counterbalanced 40-passenger cars pulled by an electrically driven steel cable. The railway has a 79m tunnel – the steepest in the world. The first carriages were wooden with defined 1st and 2nd class compartments. They were in use for over 50 years until they were retired in 1977 and replaced with the new red carriages we rode in 1978, complete with fans and automatic sliding doors.

*Penang Hill, 1978*

*Penang Hill, 1978*

**Dianne:** *Then onto Snake Temple – a Hindu temple with snakes hanging about beams and statues bringing good luck to the temple. Mark and Julian were very brave and had them wrapped around their necks but I was a chicken. We then headed home around the island – very windy, hilly road through rubber plantations, neat villages and rainforests.*

*Snake Temple*

**Julian:** *Then on to the Snake Temple. I had photographs taken with these horrible things draped round my neck. Some kind of Vipers. Becky and Dianne almost got round to touching them. We returned to Batu Ferrengi round the other side of the islands. That night a small difference of opinion concerning the washing and I got a bucket of Napisan poured over me.*

*Dad and Mark with snakes (I was a chicken, too, Dianne!)*

### Day 96 (Thursday 2nd February) – A Near Miss

**Julian:** *Well, after the night before I just had to do the clothes wash. Took me hours. Amid swims and eating we gradually tidied up, put the carpet back in and packed up. Eventually after saying goodbye to Stella and Nigel we left at 4:00 PM. First of all, went to chemist for disposable naps and cereal. Not enough money. Then to PO to meet Dianne. She and Beck walked back to* *get naps and new sunglasses for Dianne. In the meantime, I filled in form for packages sent home and wrote postcard.*

*Then onto Swettenham Pier where the Chidambaram was berthed. Through Immigration and Customs and we drove the van down the Quay to the forward end of the ship. Long wait before loading so we had dinner on board beforehand. Three other vehicles: the Booth's Land Rover, a very old VW belonging to a very old couple and a beautiful Range Rover belonging to a Swiss gentleman travelling on his own. He offered Dianne the chance to travel with him. Loaded at 8:30. The stevedores seemed to have no idea. No one in charge, all talking and shouting at once and the slings were obviously inadequate. Unfortunately, we were first to go. Backed the van onto the sling and they put in the sandbags to protect the car.*

*Working it out afterwards the winchman was primarily to blame for what happened. The van shot up in the air at maximum speed and at deck level the winch was stopped suddenly. The van jolted and resettled in the sling at an awkward angle. Once I reached the deck, I found the driver's door stove in and was unable to open it. I was furious and the deck officer kept saying 'Calm down, I would be compensated' Haha! There was a long delay with much shifting of slings before the other vehicles were lifted on board. Several near misses but no further damage. I think we all went to bed mentally exhausted.*

**Dianne:** *Last day in Penang – really think it is a lovely island with its old colonial houses (some in disrepair). It must have been fantastic 100 years ago. Chinatown is fascinating & people are lovely. Spent morning packing and enjoying the sea. Went to town in the afternoon to buy last minute things and send parcels home. Boarded ship at 6 pm. Had a lovely dinner and cabin is great. Cars were loaded on at about 9 PM. Toyota was the first and it was horrible. Was picked up in a net and the crane jerked and damaged the driver's door & dented It and bent the step so you can't open the door – very upsetting.*

*The camper being loaded onto the Chidambaram (we nearly lost it – hence the blurred photo!)*

### Day 97 (Friday 3rd February) – The Chidambaram

**Julian:** *Our cabins weren't bad. We had two three berth fairly spacious cabins with attached toilet and shower. Becky, me and Peter and Andrew were in one, with Dianne, James and Mark in the other. They would have been classed as a luxurious in their heyday. The ship had originated in the French Line and was named the Pasteur. She was only built in 1967 and handed over to the Indians in 1973. I got the feeling she really was a beautiful ship before, but now was being allowed to fall into disrepair. The decor in the 1st class saloon, dining room and smoking room was still superb but outside the decks needed attention and repair. I'm sure a good coat of paint over everything would have made a difference.*

*I saw the captain first thing in the morning. Very sympathetic about the car but nothing he could do and no compensation. The dockers and Penang Port Authority were at fault. Becky assaulted by the doctor and was told she had been reported at Penang as having 'Leprosy'. Apparently, he had to check on the report and put in a report stating she hadn't. Anyway, Beck got really upset about it.*

*We didn't do much apart from eat. I pulled out a few dents on the car and had a swim. Calm sea and the ship very steady. Arranged with captain to see the bridge the next day. Food was adequate, some Indian, some European. We had been advised to go cabin class before we booked. Dormitory and bunk class were herded together at the back of the ship, not able to use any of the facilities and barred physically from the 1st class area. The food down there apparently was terrible. Curry, very hot, and rice all the time. Apparently 36 first class passengers and 683 dormitory and bunk class passengers all herded together like animals.*

*Leaving Penang*

**Dianne:** *Breakfast at 8.30 & huge meal. Then walk about the deck & visiting swimming pool which was being filled. Lunch was another big meal. Slept in afternoon waking up in time for afternoon tea & then played backgammon. Dinner enormous followed by Yahtzee in the evening. Becky was examined by the Indian doctor who said she had leprosy (VERY STUPID)!*

Dad's entry regarding conditions on board the Chidambaran was ominously prophetic. On Tuesday 12th February 1985, a blaze destroyed the upper deck of the ship, killing 40 people. She was about 310 miles east of the Indian coast, carrying 702 passengers and 186 crew members. When she arrived in Madras two days later charred bodies were found floating on the flooded upper deck. Apparently, the fire started in the passengers' living quarters, and was most likely caused by a cooking stove, which were not permitted on board. The ship was so badly damaged that it was scrapped.

**Day 98 (Saturday 4th February) – 'Leprosy'**

**Julian:** *First thing in the morning the doctor was round demanding to know why Becky hadn't collected the cream for 'The spots on her bottom' or the 'Pigmentation in her face'. She went down there later and waited while all these dark faces pushed in front of her. She then lost her temper and got really upset. I complained to the Purser and to the Doctor. In afternoon we were shown around the Bridge. Captain gave presents to all the kids. A little bit more motion to the ship today. In the evening played cards and drank spirits.*

I remember that the Captain of the Chidamburam gave us kids presents when we visited the Bridge. Dad thinks it may have been a ploy to pacify us for the damage done to our camper van. I was given Meccano and I remember being jealous of Mike's battery powered tank and Mark's toy gun – what gratitude!

**Dianne:** *Ship life continues to be lazy – sleeping, reading, swimming, drinking and of course eating.*

**Day 99 (Sunday 5th February) – Mid Ocean**

**Julian:** *All felt very lethargic today. Nothing much doing. Bought our duty-free drinks and cigs. Quite a bit of movement on the boat today and swimming pool quite rough. Anyway, some of us went in for a swim to liven us up. Did some packing in evening and went to bed at a reasonable hour.*

**Dianne:** *Little bit rougher today. Went for a short swim but the pool was like the ocean so not good. Got ready to leave tomorrow.*

*On board the Chidambaram*

# PART IV
# INDIA
*(3,736 miles)*

~

*India: Our route from Chennai Port to Calangute Beach*
*to Mumbai to Delhi to Nepal to Lahore.*

Map © 2025 Google

Chapter Fifteen

# Madras to Bangalore

*Monday 6th – Sunday 12th February 1978*

A fter four days sailing across the Indian Ocean, we docked at Madras (now Chennai) in India. We were to spend 2 months here, the longest period in any one country of our whole trip, and covering nearly 4,000 miles. Our route took us across India via Vellore and its missionary hospital run by an old family friend, Ruth Mansfield, to the hippy community of Goa's beaches and then up the west coast to Bombay (Mumbai). We continued on to Delhi, where the van springs failed and we had to wait for new ones, after which we headed to Nepal, where we bid farewell to Dianne who went trekking. This was followed by a fraught journey back to Delhi, before heading into Pakistan.

### Day 100 (Monday 6th February) – Arriving in India

**Julian:** *Up early with land appearing on the horizon just as daylight was breaking. On journey clocks had gone back two hours. Got car packed and had breakfast as ship was docking. Around 8am went through immigration on board and then found cars weren't going to be unloaded until 12pm. Waited around for hours. Booths went ashore and had their hand baggage approved by Customs. Thought we would do it all at once when car went through. Just as well because Denise and boys then got stuck on other side with their baggage until cars were off-loaded. At least we were able to wait in air-conditioned*

137

*comfort of the ship. Van was damaged again. The other old VW swung into it when it was being offloaded. Nothing we could do about it.*

*Long wait in Customs shed before someone came to inspect the cars. They were having their lunch. Luckily, we did not have to unpack anything, but they put all our valuables on our Passports such as radio cassette, watches, calculator* [apparently to prevent smuggling, black markets and not paying taxes]. *Then had a shock when they demanded 350 RP for port dues. Left mid-afternoon in thoroughly fed-up mood and followed the Booths to the YMCA to camp. Enclosed area with grass and masses of other overlanders, mainly Swiss and German. Henri the Swiss fellow came over that evening and Becky 'persuaded' him to ask Dianne to go along as passenger. Dianne was thrilled at the prospect, and they decided to do a trial run the following day to see a couple of temples south of Madras.*

**Dianne:** *Arrived at 7 AM in port and through immigration by 9 AM then had to wait until 12.30 before car was unloaded. Customs was a mixed up affair and we walked through customs 2x without being checked. First impressions are good. Finally got car checked by 2 PM and left for campsite. Found the YMCA with no problems or at least the Booths did, and we followed. There were about 10 campers at the park – mostly Swiss and German. Henri (Swiss) came in the evening and showed us some pictures of his travels – he really has been lots of places and takes fantastic pictures. He asked me again if I wanted to go with him. There is a huge language barrier, but I said yes to a trial tour tomorrow.*

What is it about the Swiss and Germans, (the same may be said for Brits and many other Europeans), which draws them to explore? Graeme Bell, South African author, explorer and an Editor for *Expedition Portal*, explores this question in his 2019 article, which with Graham's permission I have borrowed and reproduced here:

Europeans are by far the most prolific international overland travellers. Germans and Swiss scour the planet seeking adventure and sunshine. Polish, French, Dutch, Spanish, Portuguese, British,

Scandinavians, and the occasional Belgian or Italian can be found at the furthest reaches of the globe, enjoying a glass of wine and a salad. High salaries, protective labour laws and social systems allow the good people of Europe to fulfil their dreams without compromising their future. And there would be many more families overlanding the globe if not for the restrictive European home-schooling laws – many young couples are choosing not to have children; they have dogs instead.

I remember camping near Cape Town back home in South Africa; many of the vehicles in the camp were European vehicles that housed German or Swiss couples. After seven years of extensive travel over four continents, we often shared a campfire with our European brethren and learned a few things from and about them.

### 1. Travel when you can

Over centuries, the long, cold European winters have moulded Europeans into the culture they enjoy today. We have cheese, sausage, jam, and marmalade because the Europeans learned that they had to work hard in the summer months and preserve food for the winter; a strong work ethic and community bonds ensured survival. Modern Europeans do not need to survive the winters; instead, they follow the sun south from youth to old age, enjoying glorious summers at home before returning to their overland rigs as autumn approaches. Students, as do bankers, engineers, and the white-collared masses, take advantage of the long summer holidays to travel.

### 2. Multi linguisity is an asset

It is rare to meet a European who does not speak at least two languages, and they almost all seem to speak English. The Swiss speak Swiss German, French, English, and Italian, the Germans speak French and English, and the Scandinavians need more languages to learn. Not only does this allow them to immerse into foreign cultures, but it also allows them to communicate in other languages as they have an excellent base for understanding new dialects and nuance.

### 3. Do not fear the planet or her people

Europe suffered enough war and bloodshed to learn unity and compromise. Yes, there is a rivalry between the nationalities (and the French can be maddeningly, stubbornly French), but the subcontinent is small – modern vehicles and unfenced borders allow the flow of people and ideas. It is only natural that people who do not exist in a monoculture become great travellers as they explore the planet overland respectfully.

### 4. Don't fear the cold

European campers are almost always equipped with a Planar or Webasto heater; the younger dreadlocked overlanders may even install a wood-burning stove. And though they do not particularly enjoy colder climes, they will drive across Russia in winter if necessary. Some even do it for fun. We camped with a British couple in Bulgaria (they call themselves Trucked Off). While we headed south to escape the winter, they drove their self-built Defender into Siberia in December, and Dutch LandCruising Adventures beat a similar path through ice and snow. Where there are people, you will survive, and the more hostile the environment, the more hospitable the locals are.

### 5. Eat your veggies and drink water

While South Africans grill meat, potatoes, and corn on a large campfire, our European camp neighbours enjoy a balanced meal of grains, pasta, vegetables, and fruit. And while it may seem like we have a more enjoyable meal, they are eating the healthier, cheaper meal. Ten Euros will buy roughly two pounds of meat in Morocco, while the same amount of cash will buy twenty pounds of vegetables! While we are swigging smuggled beer and burning through coal and wood, they are sipping on water and wine. Yes, we are far more interesting (and significantly larger), but they are much brighter (must have something to do with all those nutrients). What we spend in four months on food and refreshments, they spend in a year, and they can enjoy restaurant food occasionally while we simply cannot.

### 6. Everything in moderation

And I am not just talking about food and drink. Our northern cousins tend to walk the middle ground and have balanced, educated, and sensible opinions just left or right from a broad political center. Of course, we are generalising, but it is scarce to meet an extremist; they indeed do exist, but they are not travellers; they are staring at a screen somewhere in a dank room, screaming. A good night of drinking with friends ends with hugs and laughs, and everyone contributes equally to the festivities.

### 7. Modesty is admired

But man, the Swiss do not hold back when building an overland truck! And some Germans have vehicles that would make a Texan whistle. While their rigs may be OTT, the inhabitants are friendly, curious, hospitable, and usually charming. If anything, they are slightly embarrassed that they need so much muchness while treasuring ground clearance and indoor plumbing. And though the big riggers are undoubtedly well-heeled, they do not imagine themselves to be better than anyone else on an existential level – the population of Europe is majority middle class and therefore well equipped to relate to each other.

### 8. Never miss a chance to sit in the sunshine

In Africa, we have a saying – 'Only mad dogs and Englishman go out in the midday sun.' While us pale Africans are sweating in the shade, the English, French, Swiss, Germans, Belgians, Dutch, and Italians are eating lunch and drinking aperitifs under a glaring sun.

They seem to have the ability to absorb radiation and store it deep down inside, to be released as the mercury drops.

Europeans like to laugh, eat, drink, be merry, live well, and travel well.[1]

## Day 101 (Tuesday 7th February) – Children's Hospital

**Julian:** *Dianne got away early with Henri in his 'super-duper' Range Rover about 8:30. Took us several more hours to get sorted out. Eventually got off in the car and made our way to the Tourist Bureau. James and Mark stayed and played with Russell and Mike* [the Booth's sons].

*Got a map and literature about Madras, then went on to find the university where we hoped to find a doctor from the department of child health (one of Dianne's contacts) to look at Andrew's neck. We had noticed this lump on the right side of his neck on board the ship and were pretty worried about it as it was enlarging noticeably day by day. After much asking about, we eventually decided she must be based at the Children's Hospital.*

*After ice cream and a visit to the PO (one letter from Pam and John) arrived back at camp. In afternoon went by rickshaw to take Andy to child hospital. We thought the poor chap would never make it* [the rickshaw rider, not Andy]. *The doctor we wanted to see was away on holiday, but we eventually saw another. Gave us tablets without even examining Andy and said it was Cervical Adenitis. Not very impressed. What a hospital! Old and dirty with thousands of sick little Indians crying pitifully. Facilities seemed pretty limited.*

*Took taxi to the AA where we got a route map. Went over road to arrange car insurance and then back to tourist office to get our liquor licences. Got four bottles of beer costing us well over 20 Rp* [15.7 Rp to the £GBP in 1978] *at Spencers, after which we returned by taxi to camp with all our wares. Dianne decided not to travel with Henry because of his 'Ultimatum'.*

Alcohol laws in India are diverse and complex, with each state setting

---

1   Graeme Bell. 'What have we learned from European Overlanders?' *Expedition Portal*, 2019. https://expeditionportal.com/what-we-have-learned-from-european-overlanders/

its own rules concerning the legal drinking age, selling hours and types of permissible alcohol. Some areas, like Bihar, Gujarat, Mizoram, and parts of Manipur, have completely prohibited alcohol. The legal drinking age can range from 18 to 25 years, and the sale of alcohol may be government-controlled or privatised, depending on the state. The illegal consumption of alcohol in India, depending on the state law, can lead to hefty fines, jail time or community service. Hence, unless you are teetotal, (which my parents most certainly were not), as a traveller in India it is advisable to obtain a liquor licence enabling you to carry and drink alcohol legally.

**Dianne:** *Left with Henri for Mahabalipuran at 9 AM. First, we went the wrong way heading for Bombay. Went through the slums of Madras – bullock carts and people everywhere. Finally turned around and headed out of town. Passed by the beach crowded with fishermen in their dhows. Got into the villages which were mud huts with thatched roof and very clean. Mahabalipuram is a beautiful town and use to be a port of Pallavas. Beautiful carved rock shrines with village scenes. Guides everywhere and beautiful school children in colourful sarees.*

*Continued on to Kanchipuram. Fantastic countryside that was very dry with palm trees. Stopped on roadside to see farmer separating wheat with cattle walking over the stalks and pooing and peeing all over it. Then another stop to see the irrigation system with an oxen pulling wheel up from well continuously moving around in a circle encouraged by the owner. Potter also working by the side of the road.*

*Outside Kanchipuram is Thirukagkuhkudram which is a temple on a hill where they feed kites everyday which fly to Benares daily. We walked all the stairs to the top – similar to the Batu Caves. Visited many of the huge carved temples which were fantastic. Outside the temples they have large wooden carved structures covered in straw and decorated with flowers that are used in festivals and pulled through the streets. Also, there were budgie birds that tell your fortune. On the way back to the campsite, we drove over grain that was laid on the road – mechanical separation of grain by cars!*

*Meeting the people of Tamil Nadu*

## Day 102 (Wednesday 8th February) – Christian Medical College Hospital, Vellore

**Julian:** *Got packed up fairly efficiently and away by 9am. Had to go to PO and collect insurance certificate before leaving Madras. Roads were adequate though somewhat rutted. Fascinating rural scenes of mud huts, rice farming, hay carts being pulled by oxen and general idleness. Often one saw the wheat spread out on the road to be de-hasped by the tyres of vehicles. People and bullock carts everywhere in the villages. One just had to drive on one's horn continuously.*

*Fairly slow drive to Vellore. Had late lunch in the CMCH grounds. Ruth Mansfield was involved in an open-heart case, and we had to wait several hours before seeing us. She kindly got us booked into the hospital annex and arranged for us to see Sheila Pereira the next day with Andrew. We then returned with her to her cottage for tea and then got settled into our rooms.*

*Rural scenes en route to Vellore*

**Dianne:** *Up early and headed for Bangalore* [now Bengaluru] *and on the way we decided that Andrew's lump was getting bigger so decided to go to Vellore to see doctor. Interesting countryside – very flat with large hills of stones. Found the CMC Hospital with no problem – huge hospital and famous in India & the Middle East. Dr. Ruth Mansfield is a fantastic person. She's about 69 years and came to the CMC when she retired and I'm sure is working harder now than ever with open heart surgery at least once a week. She is really amazing, running about non-stop. CMH is also an interesting place started by an American missionary in 1918. Vellore practically revolves around the hospital and its auxiliary organisations. Went to the market which had huge number of stalls selling gleaming brass pots.*

Ruth Mansfield was a retired Anaesthetist known to my paternal grandfather, ('Grumpy' to us grandchildren), who every year spent some time out in Vellore helping out. As a chest physician Grumpy had worked with Ruth and told us to look her up. Dad confirms she was full of life, a bundle of energy and she really helped us out at a difficult time.

*Vellore Sunset*

*Sri Jalagandeeswarar Temple,*
*Vellore Fort*

*Walk up College Hill with Ruth Mansfield*

## Day 103 (Thursday 9th February) – Good Work

**Julian:** *After early breakfast saw Sheila Pereira at 8.0 am. Andrew was started on Erythromycin. We then went on tour of the hospital and saw Occupational Therapy, Physiotherapy, Kitchens, Laundry, Artificial Limbs and Theatres. I was very impressed. Seemed they were doing some very advanced work with minimal facilities. Went out with Ruth to eat 'Rockets' [see Dianne's explanation below] at a nearby den for lunch. In afternoon went to see the Fort and then out to the college. Saw a home for Quadriplegics and a leprosy community to help victims*

146

*get back to a normal life. Walked up College Hill to see the sun setting and then back to Ruth's for dinner.*

**Dianne:** *Tour of Vellore by Dr. Mansfield. First was hospital with over 2000 beds. Then out to lunch for a Rocket dossi which is like a 1 1/2 foot long rolled crisp pancake with curried potato inside and was delicious. Then to the Medical College a large granite building covered with local stone and bougainvillea everywhere. Climbed up College Hill to see the sunset which was beautiful – red hills, green rice paddies and reflection of sun in the water. To Dr Mansfield's for delicious dinner.*

### Day 104 (Friday 10th February) – Orphanage

**Julian:** *Late up and odd jobs in the morning such as washing. Went to town around lunch. Really hot and we were trying to find an optician. After an age of walking with Andrew bellowing, we disappeared into a den like cafe. A small dark stuffy hole smothered in smoke, and we tried to order with Andrew and Peter having top gear tantrums and throwing water all over the place. If there had been an international airport in Bangalore [Bengaluru], I think I would have flown home there and then.*

*Mum, Dianne and Andy in Rickshaw, Vellore, Tamil Nadu*

*After a disgusting snack I took three of the kids back while the others went on to the optician. Cashed more money and was just sorting out the car when*

147

*the others arrived back in a rickshaw. After tea with Ruth went out to a local pottery and were given a demonstration of potting Indian style. Quite an art.*

*Had afternoon tea at a farm and then went to see the King Home for orphaned children. Some lovely little children there and one baby. Becky immediately wanted to adopt one kid. An American missionary couple were managing the home temporarily. The Dowry System appeared in many cases to be the causative factor of orphaned children. Silk farming helped to bring in the supportive money for the home and Mulberry bushes were growing everywhere for the worms to feed on. We returned to the hospital annex to a miserable tea of curried stew.*

*Pottery making in Vellore, Tamil Nadu*

*King's Family Village Farm Orphanage*

**Dianne:** *Morning doing odd jobs in hotel. Then in afternoon went out to Keridhari which is an orphanage started by a sister at the hospital. Run on the Foster Parents basis with sponsor parents and has 98 children most of whom have been deserted. Also went to the pottery works which was similar to the one seen already. Another exhausting day and difficult to keep up to Dr. Mansfield and everyone was tired especially the kids when we got to dinner.*

The Dowry System involved the bride's parents giving the bridegroom and his relatives land, money or goods for the privilege of marrying off their daughter. It was a real burden which many poor families could not afford, causing friction, with marriages breaking down and children being abandoned.

The orphanage was founded in 1969 by Pauline King, an American missionary and it still exists today.[2] Pauline's philosophy was, 'I may not be able to do much, but I can do something. And, if I do what I can, maybe others will help.' She managed the Family Village Farm until her retirement in 1988 and through it transformed the lives of thousands of poverty-stricken people without hope. Ms. King worked for many years as a professor and public health nurse with our acquaintance Ruth Mansfield, at the Christian Medical College and Hospital. Ms. King was honoured with the President's Award for meritorious service to the community, one of the highest honours bestowed to India's citizens.

## Day 105 (Saturday 11th February) – To Bangalore [Bengaluru]

**Julian:** *Saw Sheila Pereira again at 8:0 am. Andy's lump much reduced in size. Got more medicines from pharmacy including Mycostatin cream for Andy's Monilia* [fungal infection/nappy rash]. *Away about 11am. Not a long drive but slow to Bangalore. What fun trying to find the YMCA. Backwards and forwards, everyone pointing us in different directions. Eventually found one branch but wrong one for camping. Allowed to camp at another one in Infantry Road. Small area between three walls of the building. Toilets and showers were typical Indian style with only the odd tap working.*

---

2 Mudhiyor Balar Kudumba Grama Pannai (MBKG Pannai) http://mbkgpkasam.org/

**Dianne:** *To the market early to get food. Amazingly cheap. Bought 2 kg of potatoes, 1 kg onions, 1/2 kg peas, 1 med cabbage, 1 kg carrots, 1/2 kg tomatoes all for less than $1.00 CAN. Finally, after our usual fooling around we left for Bangalore. Road was not very interesting – hills of large boulders and paddy fields and small towns which looked very poor. Bangalore is very impressive with large buildings and gardens everywhere. Camping at the YMCA and we are the only ones- so quiet and peaceful. Interesting mottos and notices everywhere: 'Work more and Talk Less'(on a truck), 'Urinals will be prosecuted (on a building), 'If you drive like hell you'll get there for sure' (on a truck).*

### Day 106 (Sunday 12th February) – Sightseeing in Bangalore [Bengaluru]

**Julian:** *A day of looking around Bangalore, the capital of Karnataka (Mysore) State and the so-called Garden City. A few nice blossoms around but it was very very dry. Walked around Cubbon Park and had a ride on a miniature train. A hot day and everyone feeling 'niggly'. Walked up to a superb British colonial building called the Vidhana Soudha or 'Secretariat', made of sandstone. It seemed such a shame that the building was being left to fall into decay and not used to full potential. We then found our way to Lalbagh Gardens where we had lunch. Marky dropped a jar of jam. After lunch we looked around the gardens, saw a pretty useless aquarium and met a mad Canadian 'Cowboy' who was trying to make a go of it in India as a Carpenter. Then back to the YMCA for dinner and bed.*

*Indian family*

*Religious procession,
Bangalore*

*The Vidhana Soudha*

**Dianne:** *Sightseeing in Bangalore. Woke up to the sounds of all the men at the YMCA clearing their throats in unison – puts you off breakfast forever. Lovely and cool in the morning – really nice climate here. First went to kiddie's playground and then to the Secretariat Building which is a huge white impressive structure with gold eagle on the top – the Parliament for this area. Then onto the botanical gardens where we had a picnic and walk – everything is very dry but bougainvillea are lovely. Met a Canadian couple in the park – he was tall lanky man wearing a huge white Stetson and cowboy tie – really unusual looking.*

Though it looks British colonial, Dad, the Vidhana Soudha was actually built between 1952 and 1956 after India's independence from Britain in 1947. The foundation stone was laid by Jawaharlal Nehru, the first Prime Minister of India, on 13 July 1951. In fact, the final design was intended to dwarf the British-built Attara Kacheri, currently the seat of the Karnataka High Court, opposite the Vidhana Soudha.

## Chapter Sixteen
# Bangalore to Goa Beach
### *Monday 13th – Sunday 19th February*

This is our mother's birthday week – Happy Birthday for Friday 17th February Mum. We wish with all our hearts you were still with us. Writing up the trip diary this week has brought you closer and I love the culmination of the week, with you and Dianne nearly dying of laughter at our campsite! That's what I remember best about you Mum – your raucous and infectious laugh (which I've been told on more than one occasion that I've inherited).

### Day 107 (Monday 13th February) – Srirangapatna

**Julian:** *Away at a reasonable time and made our way to the Tourist Office which wasn't open yet. Made our way down to Handloom House where we bought some rather lush blue silk for a shirt for me, two silk scarves and several tablecloths. Back to the Tourist Office where with great difficulty we wangled two brochures out of them but no maps. Made tentative enquiries about gas but it appeared a long drawn out procedure, so we left it.*

*Then a bumpy ride to Srirangapatna, an interesting inland fortress just before Mysore. It was from here that Tipu Sultan in alliance with the French held up the British for so long but in 1799 was eventually defeated. We looked around the Sri Ranganath Temple and saw the dungeon where British officers were tortured. The whole town was situated within the walls of the fortress. Bought a sandalwood box for 7.50 [48p] which we later discovered wasn't sandalwood.*

*I found the place fascinating. They were preparing for a festival the following day and a sense of excitement pervaded the place. A huge temple on massive wooden wheels was being prepared to be pulled through the streets by hundreds of people hauling on two chains. Masses of beggars were around, some really rather pathetic, immobile, lying on these makeshift moveable trolleys, pushing themselves along with one operational limb. That night we found a Travellers Bungalow nearby, set in some rather gorgeous surroundings near a river.*

*Collecting water en route to Sravanabelagola*

**Dianne:** *Drove onto Srirangapatna which is about 16 km from Mysore. It is a walled fort on an island – river is dry now. Its a lovely old fort with the town inside. It used to be a fort of Tipper Sultan who ruled most of Karnataha province and joined with the French to fight the British in 1799. Went to the dungeon and temple which has a reclining statue of Vishna. They are having a festival tomorrow, so the festival cart is out and being decorated. Stopped at a toy shop along the way that had beautiful wooden toys. Camped at a Tourist Bungalow nearby which is a beautiful old house and very private.*

**Day 108 (Tuesday 14th February) – Tippu's Palace**

**Julian:** *Packed up and went back to Srirangapatna to see how the festival was* *going. Masses of people, very colourful and gay with everyone in their best clothes and shouting their wares. The beggars were out in force and people were queueing in their hundreds to be blessed in the temple. We really wanted to see the huge monstrosity of a temple on wheels being pulled through the streets but no-one had the foggiest idea when. We visited Tippu's Mosque at the other end of town and then left town to see Daria Daulat, Tippu's old summer palace. Some beautiful murals depicting Tippu's battles with the British and a museum. The gardens were well kept and the grass actually green. Still no movement of the monstrosity, so after another look around we moved off to see what we could find in Mysore.*

*Saw the Maharaja's palace from the outside and then made our way to the sandalwood factory where we had a picnic lunch. After the sandalwood factory went to see the silk factory with thousands of machines clattering away pulling and winding the thread and then weaving into beautiful Saris. Dianne bought some material, and we got a fantastic Sari for Beck for 308 RP. Saw the cocoons and how they got the silk off them. Silk farming is apparently very profitable in India, especially with Government support. Had coffee and ice cream in town and then set out on a slow and bumpy ride towards Sravanabelagola camping in the grounds of a guest house at Channarayapatra where we actually had hot water.*

*Tipu Sultan's Mosque and Summer Palace*

*At Tipu Sultan's Mosque and Summer Palace*

**Dianne:** *Went into Srirangapatna again to see if the festival had started – lots of people and more like a fair then religious festival. No one seem to know when the processions is – everyone you ask you get a different time. Went to the Sultan's Mosque with its twin minarets. It must have been a beautiful place originally, but a bit run down now. Went to the Sultan's Palace which is beautiful (Darya Doulat) with all the walls completely decorated with battle scenes and frescos – very colourful. Then trip back to fort to see if cart had moved but no luck. So, we continued to Mysore where we went through a sandalwood factory and silk factory. Really interesting to see the silk stripped off the cocoons. Decided to continue on to Channaragapatna to stop the night – must make some effort getting north.*

## Day 109 (Wednesday 15th February) – 1,000-year-old statue

**Julian:** *After packing up we travelled on to Shravanabelagola to see the towering statue of Gomateswara erected in 981 AD* [the 'Willy Buddha' to Mark and I]. *Every 12 years bucketfuls of honey ghee, milk, etc are showered on the statue from a helicopter in the spectacular Mohamostak Abhisheka festival. We had to climb hundreds of steps up a rockface of a hill to see this image, but it was worth it and we got a good view of the town. A priest was making offerings at it's feet.*

*Then onwards back to Channarayapatna before progressing, but the roads weren't good so we didn't make fast progress. Eventually stopped in some town to change money and the van was immediately surrounded by peering faces. We pressed on bumping up and down but dusk was falling as we approached Jog Falls, so we stopped at a Travellers Bungalow nearby on a hill and camped in the grounds.*

Carved from a single block of granite in the early 980's the Gommateshwara statue, at 57-feet high, is one of the tallest monolithic statues in the ancient world, voted one of the Seven Wonders of India in 2007. Dedicated to the Jain figure Bahubali the statue symbolises peace, non-violence, sacrifice of worldly affairs, and simple living. It's 12 yearly ritual bathing (next in 2030) in milk, saffron, ghee, and sugarcane juice (ishukrasa) has been credited with the statue's fresh appearance.

**Dianne:** *Morning sightseeing of Shravanabelagola – famous Jain religious centre. Walked up hundreds of stairs (457 feet) to see a 17-metre stone carving built in 981 AD. Then on toward Jog Falls. The road was full of potholes so really bumped along 193 KM – very tiring. Lots of very poor villages along the way. Stopped outside Jog Falls.*

Dad mentions 'Travellers Bungalow' several times. Also known dak bungalows, these were government buildings in British India, built under British East India Company rule. They provided free accommodation for government officials and, with their permission, cheap lodging for other travellers. Dak bungalows have their origins in a tradition of guesthouses erected by Indian rulers for both Hindu and Muslim pilgrims.

*Steps to and statue of Gomateswara*

## Day 110 (Thursday 16th February) – Goa Beach

**Julian:** *First port of call was the Jog Falls which really were a bit of a disappointment considering they were the highest falls in India 253 metres tall,* [sorry Dad, I know you couldn't just Google it on your smart phone then, but 3rd highest after the 335m Nohkalikai Falls in Meghalaya, and the 310m Dudhsagar Falls in Goa], *but it was the dry season. Apparently once every month they opened the flood gates and let fall the flood over the falls.*

*What a road onward from the falls, up and down, round and round, left and left and right and right. I think we covered 50 miles in 2½ hours. The road gradually improved and we soon met the coast and turned north. The terrain was still very undulating but more open and we passed some superb looking beaches stretching out below us.*

*We passed a number of very dark and pretty girls dressed in bright costumes with masses of beautiful beads round their necks, carrying firewood on their heads. We had great difficulty in persuading them to let us take their pictures. They seemed exceptionally shy. We never did find out who or what they were. We were told either gypsies or of religious significance.*

*Opportunistic van wash*

Dad, these beautiful ladies were most likely Halakki-Vokkalu, an indigenous tribe of Karnataka State who live predominantly in the Uttara Kannada district we were driving through. Known as the 'Aboriginals of Uttara Kannada', the women adorn themselves with beads and necklaces, heavy nose rings and distinctive clothing. They speak a different dialect of Kannada called Achchagannada. According to *Travel Karnataka* the ancient customs are dying out. Literacy and exposure to urban lifestyle has led the younger generations to abandon the traditional colourful attire and sadly this may be the last generation of women to proudly wear the clothing.

*Women in Karnataka State carrying firewood*

159

*Late in the afternoon we came to a ferry crossing. In fact, we missed the turning and started up the partially completed bridge across the inlet which ended in mid-stream much to the laughter of everyone. The ferry consisted of two pontoons joined by several boards and surmounted by two planks. Quite a dicey operation. Anyway 7 of us plus the car cost 4 RP 50. We met an elderly English couple travelling in a VW. They had been waiting 3½ hours, so we were lucky to get on with them.*

*Dicey ferry across the Kail River*

*Even so it was 2 hours before we were on our way again with no mishaps. Passed into Goa where we filled in the 'Visitor's' book. After landing again we had picked up a French hippie hitchhiker who was travelling to the beaches as well. Soon after entering Goa, we tried to stop at a Forestry Travellers Bungalow, but we could not find the range officer. The elderly couple turned back to the police station, but we proceeded onwards into the night much against our principles, but we were keen to wake up on the beach.*

*Many tired hours later we arrived at Calangute Beach, Bagar end, and eager to get camped charged onto the sand only to get stuck. An hour later after many fruitless attempts at extricating ourselves and the van at a crazy angle down to the axle we pitched camp in the middle of the sand and after a midnight swim flopped at 12.45am. What an introduction!*

**Dianne:** *Went to Jog Falls first but disappointing since they only open the dam once a month and we had missed it so there was just a little trickle of water. It* *would be fantastic if the water was flowing. We continued onto Goa – up over the hills with a beautiful view of the gorge and river below. Our drive passed through lush green fields and saw some fascinating women working – they wore short sarees with lots of beads and bracelets and very shy. We tried to take their pictures 3x before finally one agreed. They also are working + + – carrying things and don't even stop to look at the van.*

*Almost drove over an unfinished bridge – really amused the Indians. Had to take a ferry across to Goa State – really just a plank on 2 small boats but no problems getting across and very lucky not having to wait because there were other overlanders in front of us who had been there for 2 hours. On the other side a French fellow asked us for a lift to Goa – he was in India converting to Hinduism. We were hoping to stop earlier but no rest houses so ended up driving all the way to Calangute Beach as the French guy knew the way. Then we got bogged – really bogged on the sand and couldn't move so just went to bed and waited for daylight.*

### Day 111 (Friday 17th February) – Mum's Birthday

**Julian:** *Becky's birthday and what we thought was going to be a terrible day. We eventually got out of the sand with the help of some metal tracks lent to us by another Overlander. With much digging and jacking up of the van we dragged ourselves free. After packing up completely we went to Calangute and had superb meal out of Prawns and Chips and Chicken and Chips with four bottles of beer. Made us feel somewhat sleepy. Did some shopping in town and returned to pitch camp properly in another location. We put the Annexe out which increased our space and made a good place for sitting out with the groundsheet underneath. After another bottle of beer and dinner we retired to bed at a reasonable hour compared to the night before.*

**Dianne:** *Becky's 30th BD. First thing was to unbog the car. Some people from the campsite helped which was good because it was really deep. There are about 10 overlanders camping at this spot – one interesting Dutch family who have 2 kids and 7 months pregnant with 3rd and planning on having her baby in Kashmir. They are travelling for a year and do this every few years with their*

161

kids. *Decided to stay by the beach to be near the other overlanders. The English couple from the ferry are also here. Out to lunch to a lovely place on the beach front. Bamboo mats on the wall and floor. Beautiful prawn and chips and beer. Then to market and back to our camp with beautiful beach in front of us.*

### Day 112 (Saturday 18th February) – Repairs

**Julian:** *As far as I can remember we had a pretty lazy day. A bit of sorting out here and there and a bit of work on the camper such as fixing wing mirrors which rotated, and bending back wheel arches. In the evening we had Joan and Bertie and Christian round for drinks.*

**Dianne:** *Relaxing day by beach – just beautiful here. Would love to stay a month.*

### Day 113 (Sunday 19th February) – A surreal day

**Julian:** *A morning of doing little. Blew up the tyre for the kids. Busloads of people came round wanting to buy things. Made about 100 RP on spare film, flash cubes, steri-strips and odd things. James and Mark did quite well selling off guns that didn't work and matchbox cars with broken wheels. After lunch we walked along the cliffs to the next beach where a flea market was being held. The beach, like Bagar and Calangute, was really lovely, palm fringed with white sand. In spite of warnings to the contrary many people totally discarded their clothes and lay exposed to the elements oblivious to everything and much to the amusement of the boys.*

*These further beaches, not so much Calangute, were real hippie colonies and this was brought home to us when we reached the flea market. We felt totally out of it and in some respects intruders. Words cannot really describe the scenes of that market. The sights, the smells, the variety of way-out clothing some of it practically non-existent, consisting of a single fig leaf fragment of clothing covering the vital spot; delicious aromas of cooking food, squalor, gaiety, Europeans mixing freely with Indians, half the people on a 'trip', all set amongst the palm trees on the edge of the beach.*

*As we were approaching the market we were passed buy a real beauty, completely smashed, shorn head, dressed in beautiful silks, thick make-up and lipstick covering his face, he passed us with a thick sickly smile waving his arms in a slow airy-fairy fashion. We had a drink and bought some 'hash' fudge and after trying to take in something of what we saw we returned to Bagar beach, all seven of us stuffed into a three-wheeler Bemo. That night we tried the hash fudge. I collapsed with tiredness while the girls couldn't help killing themselves with laughter at the most stupid things.* [Mark and I also managed to sneek some thinking they were just sweets and as I recall, ran around the campsite like lunatics for ages!]

**Dianne:** *Interesting start to the day with about 20 locals around our campsite wanting to buy anything. After our sales we trooped over the hill to the flea market – what an experience as it was a hippie colony with both Europeans and Indians. We were definitely out of place. On the beach saw a fellow dressed in sarong with flimsy shawl and full make up and brush cut blowing kisses to us all. The market was full of many others, so it became a people watching place rather than market. Best dressed was tall fellow with fabulous straw hat with colourful ribbons & long priest type outfit with huge silver belt. Others were dressed like Genghis Khan and wife including make-up. Bought some hash browns – 6 for 6 rp, so ended the day as weird as it started laughing hilariously at everything!*

Goa's northern beaches had been home to a Hippie culture since the late 1960's, and this lasted until the mid 80's. Most 'hippies' were westerners looking to escape the rat race and just be themselves. Goa was ideal for this. At the time the northern beaches were very isolated – beautiful, vast stretches of white sand fringed with palm trees. Rooms could be rented from locals for just a few dollars a day and these free living and loving westerners were welcomed. With no mobile phones or internet, they were left to their own devices. Many felt no need to wear clothes and there were regular full moon parties where hippies and locals alike listened to live bands playing the likes of Dillon, Marley, Dire Straits and Pink Floyd. Hippies became part of the local culture and economy. Once they had soaked up

163

the sunshine and atmosphere for as long as their money lasted, they would sell their belongings at local flea markets to make enough money to buy a ticket home. While the flea markets still exist today, the hippies have largely gone. Made aware of the attractiveness of Goa's beaches, large international hotel chains began taking over the hospitality scene and as the prices went up, the hippies packed up and left.

# Chapter Seventeen
# Goa to Jaipur
## Monday 20th – Sunday 26th February

After a refreshing stay in Goa, we set off for Bombay (now Mumbai), experiencing more than ever the chaos of Indian roads and the stubbornness of it's truck drivers. In Bombay we came face to face with true masses and extreme poverty, as well as a snooty Christian Mission guest house with delusions of colonial grandeur. After repairs and re-provisioning, we headed north on a tough drive to Jaipur through monotonous, dusty plains which gradually gave way to fields of wheat and sugar cane, colourfully dressed country folk, with camels and elephants replacing bullocks. As we rose higher into the hills the scenery became one of shale and stone houses and walled cities.

### Day 114 (Monday 20th February) – On the road again

**Julian:** *After a late start we reluctantly left Bagar beach. We had enjoyed those few days. After stopping at Parsim for shopping, bank and post office (nothing from the Booths) it was getting on for 12 before we were finally on our way. Slow and jolting ride to Begaum where we met the main road which wasn't much better. Camped in the dirt at a guest house in Gotur.*

**Dianne:** *Left on road to Bombay but only got about 1/3 way there stopping at Gotur. Running into lots of towns and people +++. Also lots of colourful turbans everywhere and water buffalo with decorative clothes and beads all over them.*

*En route
to Bombay
– typical
scenery in
southern
India*

### Day 115 (Tuesday 21st February) – The blocked bridge

**Julian:** *Got away at a reasonable time but a long monotonous drive to Bombay. What struck us were the number of crashed or overturned trucks and the vast number of roadworks. Most days on the move we saw at least two overturned trucks and many more crashed or broken down ones. A lot seemed to have punctures and one got the impression many crashes were caused by the Indian's habit of wearing down tyres to the inner tube then 'pop' 'skid' 'crash'. Certainly the 'Pig Headedness' of the truck drivers was also much to blame. They hated to give way or move over for overtaking or oncoming traffic. That day one small bridge was blocked by three trucks all rammed up against each other, two going one way and one the other. Quite a funny sight really. I'm sure they just could not be bothered to give way to one another. This necessitated a detour of some 20 miles which put us behind a bit, especially on the unmade roads.*

I remember this episode; in my memory the trucks were so rammed up against one another that they had smashed each other's windscreens. I remember wondering how anyone could be so stupid.

*As for roadworks I'm sure the populace was made to dig it up and then put it back just to keep them employed. Despite all these delays we reached the mud flats and industrial smog of Bombay just as the sun was setting. There was quite an impressive bridge about a mile long over the channel to the peninsula on which Bombay stood which required a toll charge. In the outskirts of the city we*

166

*stopped to eat. It was quite dark when we set off again and with no map and only a vague idea of the direction we ventured into the unknown. After several hours of going this and that way, being told to go backwards and forwards and getting more and more fed up, we eventually got a police Jeep to lead us to the Christian mission guest house in Proctor Rd. Exhausted we set up camp and had just finished when dear Miss James happened along to say we weren't allowed to camp there anymore. Anyway, she had no choice but to let us remain although we weren't allowed to use the facilities.*

**Dianne:** *Early start and passed through interesting countryside – old mountain range which we gradually climbed with no noticeable ascent then fantastic view on the top and very steep windy road down – passed over these kinds of ranges 3x. Driving is a nightmare besides 1/2 of almost every road chopped up you have the lorries hogging the road, overtaking and pushing you off the road – really horrific. Finally arrived in Bombay at about 6 pm. Drove through smog for about 50 km before reaching the city. Then the fun began – round and round we went looking for the Christian Mission and finally found it at 9pm. Put up the tent but then were told we weren't allowed to camp but could stay the night in the guest house. I slept inside the van because of the rats at night.*

### Day 116 (Wednesday 22nd February) – Chores

**Julian:** *We packed up and moved into a room, large and spacious but very expensive considering the floor was dirty and there were bed bugs as we later found out. While Beck did the washing I mucked around with the car and mended one horn. After sandwiches in our room, we took the train to the centre of town. Went to the tourist bureau and got a whole lot of literature, then to the AA for maps etc. No correspondence there from the Booths. After that we went to Petroleum House to find out about gas. Had to get a letter of introduction before going to the refinery in the morning.*

*Had drinks at the station while waiting for Dianne to come back from the Post-Office. Two letters, one from mum and one from dad. As it was rush hour, we had an early meal out at a restaurant and returned to the Mission still surrounded by a mass of humanity.*

Dianne: *Late morning then went to town in pm to tourist bureau etc. Bombay is the 1st place where the masses of people are really noticeable, with lots of beggars and sick people everywhere. Families living under canvas covers on railway bridge or in horrible bamboo huts all piled together.*

## Day 117 (Thursday 23rd February) – Gas bottles

**Julian:** *Got packed up early and went to breakfast at 8:00 AM. How very colonial and polite. It seemed a sham with false conversation. Luckily the kids were relatively good. We were glad to get away. The stay had cost us 120 RP [£7.64], 10 RP for camping with no facilities. I should have complained.*

*Well, we made our way to the office where we were to get the letter of introduction only to find the chap didn't arrive till 10. Filled in time with drinks and eventually got the letter and directions on how to get to the refinery. After dropping Dianne at the Gateway of India to go to the Elephant Caves we made our way out of town. We had hoped we would be able to go back to the caves after filling the gas bottles but like everything in India things take a long time to get done. On top of that one of the cylinders was leaking. They were very nice and while they unsuccessfully tried to mend it we had a free lunch in their canteen.*

Previous page: *Peter with sentry at Bombay Oil Refinery – gas refill; snake charmer; and Gateway of India, Bombay*

*Eventually got away and arrived back at the Gateway of India at 3pm. Looked around, had more drinks and admired some beautiful handicrafts in a very expensive store. Left in the rush hour and took an age getting out of Bombay. Problems finding a suitable rest house and after driving several hours in the dark set up camp in the bushes on the side of the road.*

**Dianne:** *Left house after being bitten by bed bugs all night. Went to Elephanta Island which was just off Bombay with nice ferry ride there. Volcanic rock carvings with scenes of Vishnu. Has aspects of both Buddhism and Hinduism and large panels with stories and very interesting told by the guide. In the afternoon did some shopping then left Bombay for Jaipur passing the millions of people in the slums around Bombay again. Couldn't find a rest house anywhere so ended up camping in the bush.*

The Gateway of India was completed in 1924 on the waterfront of Mumbai to commemorate George V's landing and coronation as the Emperor of India in 1911. He was the first British monarch to visit India. The 26-metre-high memorial arch is made of basalt and was used as a symbolic ceremonial entrance to India for important government personnel. It is also from where the last British troops in the Army of India left in 1948, following British withdrawal from India in 1947. Today, the monument is a major tourist attraction symbolising the city of Mumbai, and a gathering spot for locals, street sellers, and photographers offering their services. Two of the five jetties located at the Gateway provide commercial ferry operations.

**Day 118 (Friday 24th February) – Slow progress and provisions running low**

**Julian:** *Apart from the noise of the trucks passing all night we were undisturbed. No peering faces and we got away at 08.15, a record for us. A monotonous and long day's drive but we only did about 240 miles. It's impossible to do long* *distances on Indian roads. Numerous hold ups and road works. Camped that night outside the grounds of a guest house about 120 kilometres before Indore, with very little petrol and food and particularly no money.*

**Dianne:** *Woke up to a forest that looks like autumn which was very lovely. Early start but very long day driving up and down the Great Gnat divide which was spectacular but got boring after a while. Not a really great day and stopped exhausted in Julwana in a pleasant rest house with lovely people.*

### Day 119 (Saturday 25th February) – A close call

**Julian:** *A slow start. We were all feeling sluggish. Important that we cash money as it was Saturday. Spent our last remaining RP on petrol which is incredibly expensive in India – 3.57 RP per litre [22p]. Tried several places to get money changed but it wasn't till Indore, which we made at 12:20 (banks close at 12.30), that we managed it.*

*Relieved we had lunch out at coffee house, had a quick look around and filled up with petrol. Met a Mission lady who gave us some idea of our onward course to Jaipur. Soon after Indore left the main road onto small roads. Couldn't say they were really bad but could only go about 30 mph on them. The van being laden too heavily up front often started up an alarming rocking motion on the bumps. Also much of the road was only wide enough for one vehicle so had to continually move off onto the dirt. The trucks obviously thought the road belonged to them so a very slow and bumpy ride. Camped in some lovely grounds of a guest house where there was a heap of sand for the kids to play in. Had our wash bag stolen there.*

**Dianne:** *Again, a long day – countryside is now flat with wheat, sugar cane – all being harvested. People wearing fantastic orange, red and pink turbans. Women wearing skirts, tops and scarves all in vivid colours. Saw elephants and camels on the roads. Again, the countryside looked like autumn. Stopped at Agar for night.*

*Level Crossing in
Rajasthan*

*Women in colourful
clothing in Rajasthan*

### Day 120 (Sunday 26th February) – Nearing Jaipur

**Julian:** *Another long day of monotonous driving. The roads worse and worse all the time. Many of the country men were now wearing colourful turbans of blue, yellow, or pink and these broke up the monotony somewhat. Also, we began to see more and more camels and elephants doing the dirty work rather than the Bullocks. We still had a fair way to go to Jaipur and decided to camp about 90 kilometres short at a guest house in Tonk.*

**Dianne:** *Different country we passed through today – very rocky. First hills of shale stone and villages made of shale. Then red rocky area and houses made in circular patterns of these stones. Colour, colour everywhere. Stopped the night at Tonk which is really a large city. Passed through city called Bindi, a walled city built up the mountain, which was spectacular.*

## Chapter Eighteen
# Jaipur & Delhi
*Monday 27th – Sunday 5th March*

Beautiful Jaipur, (the capital of Rajasthan), crazy Delhi, (capital of India), and frightening news from England. This is also the week the Toyota's springs finally give up the ghost – amongst the sightseeing, the search for a Delhi mechanic …

**Day 121 (Monday 27th February) – Elephant ride to the Amber Fort**

**Julian:** *Took a further two hours to reach Jaipur, a city built of pink sandstone. Made our way to the tourist office, had coffee, an expensive pot, in the Rajasthan Palace Hotel, posted letters and had lunch at the Circuit House. In the afternoon went out to the Amber Fort.*

*Expensive coffee at Rajasthan Palace Hotel*

*The pink sandstone
of Jaipur*

*The city had a real sense of atmosphere, in some ways quite beautiful, the pink
walls, the market stalls along the street and the roads crammed with bicycles,
trishaws, ponies, camels or bullocks with carts and the odd elephant thrown in,
mixed with thousands of motorised putt putts of various kinds. Quite unnerving
driving through all this.*

*Elephant ride to the Amber Fort*

*We parked the van next to Joan and Bertie's (small world) and paid 50 RP
[£3.18] for an elephant ride up to the Fort. A huge animal which plodded
unhurriedly along stopping every now and then to empty its bowels. Felt mighty
unsafe with the saddle swaying back and forth every time the elephant took
a step. It was a long fall to the ground especially as the elephant did insist on
walking close to a wall on the other side of which was a sheer precipitous drop.
Anyway, we made it and spent an hour or so looking around.*

*A fascinating place with passageways and rooms everywhere built in the late 16th century. Some of the rooms were really beautiful with thousands of inlaid mirrors and marble. We had a demonstration in a darkened room with a candle which was quite impressive. The kids could have had an endless game of hide and seek. We eventually bumped into Joan and Bertie and after our ride down on the elephant joined them for a cup of tea. After returning to Jaipur we looked at two places to camp and eventually settled on the Jaipur Inn. Quite a nice spot, quiet, evening meal provided if wanted and we were able to set up camp on green grass. We were the only overland vehicle although there were several other 'whites' staying at the Inn.*

*The Amber Fort, Jaipur*

**Dianne:** *Drove into Jaipur around noon – tourist bureau first then relaxing cup of coffee on the lawn of the Rajasthan Hotel – really beautiful with lawn and lovely chairs and peace. Then through old city, which is fascinating with fantastic shops, pink walls, people everywhere. Went to Amber Palace and Fort (1600). Beautiful, mirrored palace and rode an elephant from base of hill. Rather a frightening experience with 7 of us balanced on a wobbly platform 12 ft off the ground. Stayed at the back of a lovely hotel on grass and nice people but no overlanders.*

### Day 122 (Tuesday 28th February) – City Palace

**Julian:** *Beck and Dianne went shopping in the morning while I looked after three kids and tried to do some work on the car. After organising lunch and*

175

*trying to keep them happy we took a trishaw into town to meet the others at the City Palace at 3:00 PM. Exchanged $200 American dollars for 1680 RP with some European who was trying to get rid of his Rupees. The girls eventually arrived looking 'dead beat' and we dragged ourselves around the palace seeing exhibitions of arms and clothing and carpets. The palace itself was not very impressive or beautiful. Started to rain so we took a pony and cart back to the Jaipur Inn. Soon after another overland vehicle arrived. Seven of them travelling in the same van from England and back.*

**Dianne:** *Shopping in the morning. City is very different with its pink walls. Went to City Palace in afternoon which was very beautiful costume display – all golden & silver threads. Horse cart ride back to van.*

*City Palace, Jaipur*

## Day 123 (Wednesday 1st March) – Wildlife sanctuary

**Julian:** *A slow start as we were chatting to the English couple who arrived in the van that had just arrived. We were now riding very low as the shock rubbers had disintegrated and the springs were rather tired. What with the weight we were carrying, we set off rather carefully towards Delhi where we hoped we would be able to get the springs seen to.*

*Colourful Jaipur*

*Short drive to Sariska Wildlife Sanctuary which was 44 km off the main road. Set up camp at the guest house and at 5:30 PM all piled into a Jeep with several others to see what sights they were to see. Nothing much I'm afraid. No tigers or lions or elephants. Saw several 'Blue Bull', Antelopes, a Jungle Cat and many deer like creatures. A bit disappointing. Got back after dark and retired early.*

**Dianne:** *Left midday for Sariska Game Sanctuary and arrived around 2 pm. At 5pm went for a jeep trip through park – saw samba, spotted deer, wild boar,* *wild cat and blue boar but no tigers. It was lovely riding along through the forest at night and very peaceful.*

### Day 124 (Thursday 2nd March) – Delhi & Mavis sick

**Julian:** *We had to return 44 km along the same small road to take the main highway because the onward road had been washed out by heavy rain. Main road was one of the best we had been on in India. Even so it was mid-afternoon before we reached Delhi. Went to the Post Office first and collected mail. Not good news. Mav,* [Mum's mum, our 'Granny'], *was sick and was waiting to go in for a biopsy.*

*Pete & Cream Crackers with Andy eating 'Paddington Bear' at Kashmir campsite*

*Looked at the two campsites and decided to settle for the one near Kashmir gate. Although not so nice it was cheaper. Had tea out at the restaurant and then set up camp.*

**Dianne:** *Drove into Delhi – very western city and stores++. Found a campsite* *in Old Delhi.*

### Day 125 (Friday 3rd March) – Springs and circus

**Julian:** *Sluggish in morning and eventually got away to Nepalese Embassy. Visas for six of us cost RP 225 [£14.33] and would be ready the next day. Went out for dinner at Moti Mahal restaurant and had the most delicious, spiced chicken and warm bread. Cost a bomb RP 180 [£11.46] but we thought it was worth it. In afternoon looked around for garage to do the car. Not much joy. Coil springs could not be stretched and re-tensed. Possibly an inserted plate would raise the van half an inch. New springs were needed, and it was more likely we would get these in Kathmandu than Delhi. We then gave up and went to the circus instead. Not bad, certainly packed with variety. Kids loved the stunt driving of a Jeep and bike jumping over ramps. Greg and Pam had arrived at the site in the early hours of the morning, and we had them over for coffee and soup.*

**Dianne:** *After washing etc went to Nepal Embassy for visas. Then some shopping. Walked about Chadni Chow in PM and not very impressed. Went to post office to phone home but not successful but interesting to people watch with locals writing telegrams from the list of suggestions on the walls. Red Fort looks spectacular especially with thousands of sheets hanging on the fences around it – there must be a laundry nearby. Traffic unbelievable and smog even worse. Lunch at Moti Mahal which was very expensive but delicious Tandoori & 2 other kinds of chicken and then Gulap Jalan for dessert.*

### Day 126 (Saturday 4th March) – A solution

**Julian:** *Went to tourist office in morning and looked around the shops. Took silk into a tailor to be made-up into a shirt, and then rushed down to Nepalese embassy to get our visas. Returned to other campsite near Delhi Gate to enquire about facilities and have lunch there. Mechanic on premises who said he could do the job while we were living in the van. Decided to move there the next day. After eating returned to Connaught Circus and did a shop at the Empire Stores. James and Mark bought a new belt. Rushed back to camp and had a quick tea* *before going to a show of classical Indian dancing.*

**Dianne:** *Busy day. Picked up Visas. Went shopping and looking at carpets but they are unbelievable prices so don't think I can afford. Went to Indian classical dances which were really interesting. Some are very Chinese/Tibetan dances and other Indian dancers with bells on ankles and the facial expressions and make up and very enjoyable.*

## Day 127 (Sunday 5th March) – Delhi Gate

**Julian:** *Packed up slowly and moved to other campsite near Delhi Gate. Greg and Sam had also moved the day before. Soon after setting up camp the mechanic got started on stripping the suspension. Did not do much that day. Pottered around doing odd jobs.*

**Dianne:** *Moved to other campsite which was much cleaner. Mechanic started on car immediately which is terrific. Beautiful day and we washed and dried clothes and just watched other van and campers. Penn Overland and Encounter Overlanders groups are also at the camp grounds.*

Chapter Nineteen

# Delhi, Taj Mahal and Sex Temple

*Monday 6th – Sunday 11th March*

With the van springs fixed by Tuesday, and after a week in Delhi sightseeing, shopping, sorting out van insurance, visas and restocking on gas, we left for Agra and one of the Seven Modern Wonders of the World – the Taj Mahal; a truly awe-inspiring testament to the love of the Mughal emperor, Shah Jahan, for his favourite wife Mumtaj Mahal, built between 1631-1643. At the end of the week, waking at our Guest House in Nowgong Mr. Pathak, a local photographer, teacher, construction engineer and mechanic, (quite a list!), generously invited us for a delicious lunch with his family. Apparently, he had spotted us at the Red Fort in Delhi and was very keen to know more about England. After lunch, we continued onto Khurajharo – the sex temple – which featured carvings of hundreds of different sexual positions. Apparently, these sculptures helped the local boys (who lived as bachelors at the temples until they attained manhood) learn about the worldly role of 'householder'. Mark and I were certainly fascinated!

**Day 128 (Monday 6th March) – Van on stilts**

**Julian:** *The mechanic was working on the car all day which had its snoot up in the air, which made living in it rather difficult. Again an uneventful day apart*

181

*from the evening when we went to see Son et Lumiere at the Red Fort. Caught a Bemo there. Interesting but nothing really impressive.*

**Dianne:** *Went shopping again for Kashmiri carpets – still too expensive. Beginning to bargain but get so confused in the end I don't feel like buying anything. Went to Sound & Light Show at the Red Fort – really good history of Delhi and it is a beautiful Fort at night. Show was very anti-British who are portrayed as unfeeling dictators. Also, it was a very cold night.*

### Day 129 (Tuesday 7th March) – New springs

**Julian:** *In morning took the two older boys to town to arrange the car insurance. Had to go to a second office but it could have been worse. We did some food shopping and had lunch out. When we returned the van was ready. Later that afternoon we took it for a test ride out of town on a rough piece of ground. The boys loved it pretending we were a four-wheel drive pounding through the mud. I was quite pleased with the result – there was an extra 4-inch clearance above the wheels. Got back after dark, much to Beck's annoyance. Paid 725 RP [£46.15] for the job.*

**Dianne:** *Delhi belly in Delhi and its horrible. Dragged myself to Iran Embassy and then back to carpet place but decided not to buy one. Then slept between toilet visits.*

### Day 130 (Wednesday 8th March) – Bad mood

**Julian:** *All went to town. Greg and Sam left for Kabul. Collected the insurance certificate and shirts etc. Dianne was really upset with her blouse. Hung all 'groggily'. Mine was good. We had to see the Taylor again at 1pm so we looked around the shops and had lunch out at a nearby cafe. Bought some new shirts for the kids.*

*After lunch went to see the Jama Masjid Mosque. Supposed to have been the biggest and most beautiful mosque in India but we were very disappointed in it. Looks quite impressive with its spires and domes from afar but inside nothing much. Didn't go up the tower because they would not accept our 2 Rp note and wanted to charge us 2 Rp extra for the camera. Got really annoyed with them and told them we would put a complaint into the tourist board.*

*In a bad mood we went off to see the Red Fort in daylight. That wasn't very impressive either. Pearl Mosque was quite nice and then Peter poohed his pants and we missed the museum. Went back to camp having had rather a frustrating day.*

**Dianne:** *Spent afternoon sightseeing to Jama Masjid Mosque – largest mosque in India built around 1600 – usual huge sandstone structure. Then to Red Fort built by Emperor Shahjahan in 1638 and is a series of buildings in red sandstone. Must have been beautiful at one time but now pillaged and rotted so very empty. The Pearl Mosque was the best preserved.*

### Day 131 (Thursday 9th March) – Lunch at the refinery

**Julian:** *After packing up first stop was to take a picture of the washing outside the Red Fort and of Jama Masjid Mosque.*

*Left: Red Fort, Delhi (with turbans drying)*

*Below: Jama Masjid Mosque when leaving Delhi*

*Dropped Dianne there to catch a Bemo to sort out her Visa and we made a slow and frustrating drive out of town to the gas place. Having eventually found it we decided to leave the bottles there and go to the post office. Having returned at 12:00 o'clock we found they hadn't even started filling the bottles so in the middle of their yard we got out the beer and bread and had our lunch much to the amusement of the workers.*

*We were supposed to have met Dianne at a cafe at 12 but after going to the GPO in old Delhi (lucky, we did, we got a letter from Ruth Mansfield) it was pretty late before we got back to the centre of town. We then eventually made our way out south to the Qutb Minar Complex, which contained the tower, the 1600-year-old pure iron pillar that never rusts and a really old mosque and other archaeological finds. Beautiful carvings.*

*Alai Minar Tower – started by ruler Alauddin Khalji in 1300AD but never finished*

*We could have spent a lot longer there, but we had to get to Agra. Left about 3pm. Good road and we made it to Taj as darkness was falling. Caught a glimpse of the dome in the gathering dusk but there was no full moon so we didn't go in. Camped at the Highway Inn. Very friendly people and nice surroundings. Were not hassled by onlookers and James and Mark got on well with the owner's son.*

**Dianne:** *Sightseeing Qutb Minar Complex – beautiful old ruins with 13th century tower of sandstone & marble which was beautiful. Also, Quwwat-ul-Islam – earliest extant mosque – beautiful, curved columns. In the centre is an iron pillar exposed to elements for 1600 years and not rusted. Locals try to wrap their arms around the pillar and if they can it means they will prosper. Then started driving to Agra and road was good. Reached Agra about 6.30 PM and it was dark by the time we reached Taj Mahal but it still looks good – can't wait until the morning.*

The Qutb Minar complex is a collection of monuments and buildings in Delhi which originated in the construction of the Qutb Minar 'victory tower' to celebrate the victory of Muhammad Ghori over the Rajput king, Prithviraj Chauhan, in 1192 AD and was only completed in 1368. Its construction marked the beginning of Muslim rule in India. Built using red sandstone and marble, at 72.5 metres (239 ft) high, it is the tallest minaret in the world built of bricks. Inscriptions record that 27 Hindu and Jain temples were torn down for it's and the neighbouring Quwwat-ul-Islam Mosque's (Dome of Islam), construction. It was the first mosque built in Delhi after the Islamic conquest of India.

The iron pillar, erected in 402 AD by Chandragupta II Vikramaditya (375–414 AD) in front of a Vishnu Temple complex at Udayagiri was later shifted by Anangpal in the 10th century to its present location.

The pillar is 7.21-metre high and weighs over six tonnes. It was set up as a 'Vishnudhvaja', a standard of god, on the hill known as Vishnupada in memory of the mighty king Chandra. It has never rusted and as Dianne says, if locals can wrap their arms around it, they see it as a sign of future prosperity.

### Day 132 (Friday 10th March) – The Taj Mahal

**Julian:** *Dianne disappeared early to see the sunrise on the Taj. We eventually got there around 10:00 AM. Really was a very beautiful monument, probably best seen as a whole from a distance. Built in the 1630's of white marble it must have had an incredible feat of building. I was very impressed. The grounds it*

185

*was set in were well kept and clean. The inside perhaps was not as impressive as the outside. The coffins of the Emperor and his wife were laid side by side in a dark basement whilst above was the large cenotaph chamber with the two replica coffins immediately above the originals so that people would not stand above the latter. Spent some time admiring this beautiful edifice, had our photographs taken and then had lunch out at a cafe. Took hours coming.*

*The Taj Mahal*

*Then looked around the local handicraft shops and bought a bedspread. Tried to get money changed but too late so returned to camp for a cup of tea. After refreshing ourselves Dianne and I took a trishaw to the Agra Fort. More interesting than the Red Fort at Delhi it also was built of red sandstone in the late 1500s. Contained the largest all marble mosque in the world and some rather interesting apartment rooms.*

*Left Dianne to finish looking around while I went off to try and cash money in town. No luck and I was so fed up I walked back. It looked a dull over clouded evening, so I headed back to camp. Just my luck I had wanted to photograph the Taj in a setting sun and just as I was nearing camp the sun came out really brilliantly 10 minutes before dropping below the horizon. Would have been superb. The Wing Commander was having tea with the girls when I came back and the photographer returned with photographs. Really disappointing.*

186

**Dianne:** *Up at sunrise to see Taj Mahal – beautiful – no words to describe it and sat watching for an hour – watching the sun reflect off the semi-precious jewels – topaz, coral, transparent amber, agate & lots of others I can't remember – all made into beautiful flowers, tiger lily, grape vines, chrysanthemum. Really lives up to all expectations. Built 350 years ago by Shah Jahan in memory of his wife. Visit in afternoon to Red Fort which was built before the Taj (1565). Some rooms similar to Taj with marble and flowers of stones. Entrance to Fort and huge gate was very interesting and upper storey of fort with turrets along the side is very picturesque.*

## Day 133 (Saturday 11th March) – Nowgong holes

**Julian:** *Packed up really early without breakfast and went off to the Taj about 7:15 AM. Beautiful in the soft morning light, though again it was cloudy. Had a superb huge breakfast out at the cafe where we had eaten the day before and set out about 9:30 heading for Gwalior. Had some pretty heavy rainstorms as we entered Gwalior and had difficulty finding a bank. Just found one before 12:30. Carried on to Jhansi and camped in the grounds of a Guest House in Nowgong. Lots of holes in the ground and the van sunk in somewhat.*

**Dianne:** *Long drive on way to Khuraajharo. Mostly flat countryside and lots of huge rivers. We crossed one on a floating bridge which is covered with manure instead of bitumen which was very unique. Rained today and pelted down which was a pleasant change and rather cool. Made good timing and stopped at Nowgong.*

## Day 134 (Sunday 12th March) – Local hospitality

**Julian:** *One of the kids who was an onlooker brought a message from his father for us to come over for tea so after packing up we all shoved in the van and told him to take us home. It turned out the father who was a photographer had seen us at the red Fort in Delhi. After tea he persuaded us to go with him to visit a museum in the next village and then come back for a proper Indian lunch with them. He wanted us to stay as his guests for the whole day so as not to hurt his feelings too much we agreed to the former.*

*The museum was full of old uninteresting to us bits of sculpture, so we were pleased to get away. His wife did not speak any English and she cooked squatting by an open fire in the courtyard. The house was a broken-down hovel but in spite of that they were well dressed, clean and educated. We sat down in Indian style cross legged on a mat and ate chapatis, rice cabbage, potato and tomato mixture with our fingers. We appreciated the fact we had had a proper Indian meal cooked in proper Indian style over an open fire.*

*A rare photo of all seven travellers*

*We eventually made our escape and an hour later reached Khajuraho. A number of bizarre looking temples with masses of carvings of pornographic material all over them. They all looked much the same and were not all that impressive although they were set in rather nice surroundings. Didn't spend long there and carried on to camp in a somewhat deserted Guest House near Panna. They either did not have toilets or showers, or they didn't understand what we wanted.*

**Dianne:** *While packing up we were invited by one of the spectators for tea and decided to go. Mr. Pathak is a local photographer, teacher, construction engineer, mechanic. His choice question was 'Please explain bigger system in England'. Very welcoming man and invited us to dinner and would not take no as an answer. So, we went to a local museum and then back to his place for dinner which was a very good meal cooked by his wife over a wood fire. Chapatis hot from the fire cooked directly on the coals. Also boiled cabbage, rice, tomato potato dish. Not too spicy and very delicious.*

*After dinner we continued onto Khajuraho – the sex temple. All the carvings of hundreds of different sex poses were about 12 feet above the grounds so had stiff neck at the end. Drove a few miles before camping for the night.*

*Khajuraho – the sex temple*

The Khajuraho Monuments are a group of Hindu and Jain temples in Chhatarpur district, Madhya Pradesh. A UNESCO World Heritage Site, the temples are famous for their nagara-style architectural symbolism and erotic sculptures. Built between 885 AD and 1000 AD by the Chandela dynasty, by the 12th century there were 85 temples, spread over 20 km2. Of these, only 25 temples have survived. Following the Muslim invasion of 1192, the temple complex was forgotten and overgrown by the jungle until 1838 when Captain T.S. Burt, a British engineer, rediscovered the complex.

Chapter Twenty

# The Ganges, Nepal and Himalayas

*Monday 13th – Sunday 19th March*

After the wonders of the Taj Mahal and the sex temples, we moved on to Varanasi and the holy (but filthy) Ganges River where Dianne took Mark and I for an early morning river cruise to catch a beautiful sunrise and as it happened, a cremation on the riverbank. Then onto the border with Nepal, Pokhara and the free lake campsite where overlanders, trekkers, sherpas and hawkers alike congregated in the shadows of the awesome snow-capped Himalayas. Here we got rather carried away bartering some of our stuff for trinkets we thought we needed. Next stop Pokhara with its incredible mountain views, Aunt Jane's Pie Shop and Freak Street. A combination of dwindling finances and my Mum's Mum's illness meant that this was the week my parents decided to head back to England as quickly as possible.

### Day 135 (Monday 13th March) – Varanasi

**Julian:** *A reasonable start and we headed on for Varanasi. Roads were quite good and we made reasonable time. First impressions of Varanasi were terrible. It was filthy overcrowded and stunk. We spent hours forcing our way through the masses trying to find a camping ground. Eventually found quite a little community of overlanders camping at dak bungalow in a better part of town.*

191

**Dianne:** *Had a whole days drive to Benares (Varanasi) then hours to find the guest house. Benares is a huge crowded and really filthy city. The campsite is nice though.*

### Day 136 (Tuesday 14th March) – The Ganges

**Julian:** *Dianne and the boys got up at 5:00 AM and went on the tour to see the activities on the Ganges as dawn broke. Apparently quite a sight as thousands of people prayed, did yoga, washed themselves and cremated dead bodies on the shores. Here, Beck and I had a bit of a lay in and we had an intentional slow morning packing up and being lazy.*

*After an early lunch of omelettes at the restaurant we set off northwards and after 5½ hours reached Gorakhpur. The usual hour or so of looking around for a camp place and eventually squeezed ourselves into the garden of a hotel next to the wall with the usual herd looking on. Again, this town appeared exceptionally overcrowded with milling masses of trishaws, bicycles, bullock carts, pony traps and motorcycles. The chap got quite upset because we blocked up his hole with loo paper. Thought it was cotton. Said he used water* [It was usual to not use toilet paper, just water and the left hand!].

**Dianne:** *Up at 5 AM to see Ganges at sunrise. James and Mark came with me and Becky and Julian stayed at campsite. We went for breakfast at a western hotel for a treat before heading for the river. Fantastic sites. Loud music blaring from the temple. People crowding the steps to the river – begging, praying, selling flowers. The priests sitting under their bamboo umbrellas – they hold the clothes of the devotees and bless them. Then people bathing, washing, brushing teeth, washing clothes, swimming. Others doing yoga, meditation, worshipping the rising sun.*

*Sun is red ball rising over the river – colour is fabulous. Boat ride up to crematorium was fascinating. Hindus have to be cremated within 24 hours of death. They are brought to the river and bathed then the eldest mourner (eldest son, father) shaves head, baths in the river and goes to special place to buy wood. The body is covered with cloth and taken to the temple where chief mourner walks about body 5 times to release 5 spirits – air, earth, water, fire and ether. The body can then be burned and is put on fire for at least one hour after which the ashes are thrown in the river. The fires are on the steps and they were burning already, a body waiting on a step.*

*After we walked through numerous small alleys to the Golden Temple – 2 tombs with 1 ton of gold plate on it – very beautiful. Both the Temple and the Ganges are a must for every Hindu, once in a lifetime. Drove onto Gorakhpur in PM.*

*Dawn on the Ganges at Varanassi*

The Ganges is the world's second largest river delta by volume and the holy river of Hinduism – the embodiment of the goddess Ganga, cleansing bathers from their sins it is believed. It is also the dirtiest river in the world; a consequence of dumping raw sewage, chemicals, partially burned or unburned bodies from funeral pyres and animal carcasses, by a

193

consumption base of over two billion people. There are higher incidences of waterborne diseases in communities frequently exposed to this holy river, now covered with a layer of floating plastics and other wastes – over a billion gallons a day! Despite this, the Ganges is commonly used for bathing, irrigation and in houses and buildings.

Efforts to clean up the river have been ongoing since 1986 under the Ganga Action Plan, initiated by then Prime Minister Rajiv Gandhi. More recently Prime Minister Narendra Modi has poured billions into the latest round of efforts. So far, these efforts have achieved limited success. No wonder, given Hindus believe their legendary king Bhagiratha performed a tapasya (spiritual meditation) to bring down the river Ganges upon earth from heaven, so that he could immerse the ashes of sixty thousand of his slain ancestors in her sacred waters.

### Day 137 (Wednesday 15th March) – Pokhara

**Julian:** *150 km to the border. The road seemed busier than ever and up here in N India nothing seemed to move out of the way. Spent two hours at the border. All very nice but they took their time. Fascinating how over the border the* *crowds of bikes and trishaws just melted away.*

*The outline of the Himalayas which we had first glimpsed just prior to the border were now fast emerging out of the haze and quite suddenly we left the plain and entered the foothills. It was a hard slog after a late lunch, another 150 km to Pokhara. Mainly 3rd and 2nd gear work, up one range and down another, all the time going round and round curving back on oneself time and time again. No white peaks but it was lovely scenery. We were still driving when darkness fell and we only reached Pokhara about 9:30pm. Really rotten driving into a strange city at night and not knowing where the hell you're going. No one seemed to speak English. We eventually found our way to the lake where people camped free and immediately got bogged. However, we were pushed out after having to use the jumper leads, battery was flat as well.*

*Foothills of the Himalayas*

**Dianne:** *Started early and reached border by about noon. Took 2 hours to get through and then headed for Pokhara. Very windy, up and down hills and beautiful countryside with plateau gardens, red hills and blue river. Very slow going at 20KM and didn't get to Pokhara til 10 PM. No sign of snowy mountains. People very different. Passed several people carrying huge loads in baskets with strap on their foreheads.*

195

### Day 138 (Thursday 16th March) – The Himalayas

**Julian:** *A beautiful awakening. The lake hung in a hollow in the morning mist rapidly clearing with the rising sun. White peaks rearing up on one side behind the nearer mountains into a clear blue sky (they were in fact 70 miles away).*

*Salesman at Pokhara campsite*

*Sherpas were busy cooking breakfast for the Trekkers on open fires. Little dugout log canoes were manoeuvring around the lake. The night had been a bit chilly, but the day was surprisingly warm. We were soon descended upon by masses of sellers of souvenirs and getting carried away we exchanged many of our things, which we later regretted.*

For example, (Dad has just reminded me), Mark and I swapped our blow-up canoe (previously pictured) for two ornamental knives. Mine is pictured below.

*Did the washing in the morning and in the afternoon went for a walk. Turned out to be rather a long walk as the first bank we went to was closed and we had to go on to the bank at the airport. James was grizzling on the way back about being tired. Beautiful views of the snow-capped mountains. Picked up Dianne and went out to dinner and had beautiful steak – enormous helpings. Met Beryl and Trudy that day.*

*Dianne checking out the surroundings*

**Dianne:** *Woke up to excited screams from the boys of snow on the mountains. Really beautiful to look out the window and see foothills with peaks of snowy mountains behind. Relaxing day after herds of Nepalese left (trade, trade, trade). I swapped my Timex for a copper bowl – likely not a good trade but got carried away with the crowd. Rest of day reading, chatting, swimming. Really warm in the sun. Van got attacked by bull who fancied the washing on the line – rather frightening. Out for dinner – huge meal of rice, veg and meat followed by rum coffee.*

## Day 139 (Friday 17th March) – Kathmandu

**Julian:** *Late start after the evening before and we set off to Kathmandu. Road was exceptionally good after what we had come on and we did 200 km in six hours stopping for lunch. Unfortunately, we were descended on by dozens of*

197

*school children who were just leaving school. First port of call in Kathmandu was the post office then the usual hassle of trying to find a campsite. Eventually found one just below the Swayambhunath Temple. Apparently, there was no one particular place where overlanders gathered. They spread themselves around the grounds of various hotels and lodging houses. We set up camp in daylight for once.*

*Mark and I checking out our new back garden,*
*Overlanders' free lake campsite at Pokhara*

*Nepali children on the road to Kathmandu*

Swayambhunath, a Hindu name meaning 'self-sprung', is an ancient hilltop religious complex (stupa) in Kathmandu Valley consisting of a variety of shrines and temples dating back to at least the fifth century. The Tibetan name for the site means 'Sublime Trees' after the many varieties of trees found on the hill. For Newar Buddhists (inhabitants of Nepal's Kathmandu Valley) it is the most sacred pilgrimage site and for Tibetan Buddhists, it is second only to Boudha (another stupa in Kathmandu).

According to mythology, the whole valley was once an enormous lake, out of which grew a lotus flower, over which the stupa was later built. Manjushri, the bodhisattva (person on the path to awakening) of wisdom and learning, had a vision of the Lotus at Swayambhu and made the journey there to worship it. Seeing that the valley would make a good place to settle, and in order to create access for pilgrims, he cut a gorge at Chovar, draining the lake water and leaving the valley in which Kathmandu now lies. The Lotus was transformed into a hill and the flower became the stupa. While raising the hill Manjushri, going against tradition, let his hair grow long. This resulted in head lice, which eventually transformed into the holy monkeys living in the temple today.

### Day 140 (Saturday 18th March) – Wet, Wet, Wet

**Julian:** *In morning I woke to find we were somewhat washed out. An actual pool of water was lying on the top of our sleeping bag from the window which we had not shut properly. Also, the water was seeping up through the tent. Well, it wasn't actually raining then so we had a bit of a clear out before it started again, got our raincoats out during a lull and eventually set out sodden to town. Post office wasn't open so after dropping Dianne off we went for a walk and bought a few provisions such as bread, butter, eggs. Returned to post office only to have to wait another half an hour. They seemed to open it when they felt like it and when they did, we found we wanted the Telegraph Office down the road. Beck was going to have to wait one hour before getting through to home. I took over the kids and tried to keep them happy. Kept peeing with rain and Andrew was grotty.*

*Eventually met up with Dianne and Becky. Phone call had apparently been hopeless, she had had to shout, and she had had to pay an extra 40 RP for being one minute over. We weren't even sure that Charles [Mum's Dad] had fully understood what we required. Had coffee and then went looking for milk.*

*While I was fighting with locals at the dairy Beck and Dianne met up with Bob who then took us to the most delicious cake and pie shop possible, which elevated our spirits somewhat. We also bought some most delicious homemade brown bread and then returned to camp to dry out. Sun was half out so we took everything out to hang up to dry which was a mistake because immediately the sun disappeared, and it pelted down. Had afternoon high tea and that night Beck and I and kids slept in van so only Dianne would get wet. Anyway, it didn't rain anymore that night.*

**Dianne:** *Rainy and cold and everything wet wet wet. Finally got into town but closed today. Becky and Julian have decided to go home as quick as possible so I am going to go with Beryl and company if I still can. Went to 'New Pie Shop' which was fantastic with about 10 different kinds of pie. I had a sumptuous chocolate cream pie. The brown bread for tea with jam was delicious.*

## Day 141 (Sunday 19th March) – Freak Street

**Julian:** *A great drying out session in the morning. Luckily it was a beautiful morning. After hanging half our belongings around the campsite, we set out to American Express to ask their advice about forwarding money. They suggested American Express in Delhi. Then off to the Telegraph office to telegram Charles. Drastically had to reduce number of words when we found it was twice as expensive as the telephone call. Then went to get Dianne's trekking permit after which we lunched out at Aunt Jane's – good, western food and delicious apple tart. In afternoon we had a look down Freak Street and tried to sell some oddments such as clothes without much luck. Bought a couple of jumpers etc.*

**Dianne:** *Shopping day. First business was trekking permit. Then onto Aunt Janes for super lunch – hamburger and apple pie with peanut ice cream then chocolate cake with ice cream. Then shopping. Becky traded clothes for jumper and handbag which was really good.*

Freak Street, (now 'Old Freak Street'), is south of Kathmandu Durbar Square and was so named in the 1960s after hippies from around the world started travelling there in search of legal cannabis, Tibetan culture,

Buddhism and enlightenment. They were particularly attracted by the government-run hashish shops. However, In the early 1970s the Nepalese government, pressured by the US who had declared a 'war on drugs', started a round-up of hippies on Freak Street and deported them to India. They then imposed strict regulations for tourists regarding dress codes and physical appearance and banned the production and sale of hashish and marijuana in Nepal. Hippie tourism was quickly replaced by trekking and cultural tourism.

Chapter Twenty-One

# Kathmandu to Agra

*Monday 20th – Sunday 26th March*

With Mum and Dad deciding to head for home as quickly as possible, Dianne had chosen to go trekking with Beryl and Trudy who we met at the campsite in Kathmandu, so this was the week that we parted ways after ten weeks' close companionship. The week started with some mountain sightseeing, another visit to the pie shop, some questionable bartering and Nepalese dancing. Then back to Pokhara, helping an Indian family to repair a puncture on the way, arriving at the lake campsite for Dianne's final night with us. After bidding fond farewells we had a couple of days at the lake campsite for car maintenance and relaxation before heading back to India and through Uttar Pradesh to Agra on what, unknown to us, was Holi Day (and coincidentally Easter Saturday). Our ignorance of what to expect resulted in the most frightening day of our whole trip …

**Julian:** *Took a trip into the hills with Bob* [a lone traveller hitching around Asia]. *Gate was locked so we had to saw our way out. A long slow but beautiful drive up until we got the most gorgeous views of snowy mountains. Took masses of photographs and had sandwiches up there.*

*Returned to town and went to the pie shop for pudding. After that we set up stall in the marketplace and managed to sell quite a number of our baby clothes and oddments. Palmed off a faulty gas cylinder. A bit of bargaining and*

203

*exchange in Freak Street bought up more goods, such as a coat for me, a bag for Becky, coats for the boys. A good day's shopping. After coffee we went off to see some Nepalese dancing. The boys loved the Peacock dance. Came out and started kissing everyone. More action and exciting than the Indian dancing we had seen.*

Seeing the laundry bucket in the photo above reminds me of a story a family friend recounts in response to my first Facebook blog post:

> *The nappy washing machine! Your mum calculated that if she bought disposables for Andy, they would completely fill the camper, so the solution was a bucket with a lid, the motion of the van cleaned the cloth nappies as it went … !!*

**Dianne:** *Drove up nearer the mountains. Really winding narrow road but beautiful view when we got there of the Himalayas – had to rush to avoid the clouds. Back to Katmandu and out for pie – apple and lemon – delicious. Then continue bargaining – started a stall in the market but in the end had 20 people surrounding us pulling things out of our hands and shouting prices – really funny but very satisfying. Then onto dance performance in the evening – really good program with about 8 dances.*

*Nepalese dancing including the 'kissing peacock'*

## Day 143 (Tuesday 21st March) – Good Samaritans

**Julian:** *Packed up and left that morning. Dianne spent hours changing money while we did the odd jobs such as shopping for food, milk, etc and tried to do some more bargaining in the market. Not much luck this time. We had a last* *lunch at Aunt Jane's and then set out for Pokhara. Peter had the shits and James and Mark weren't feeling all that well. Stopped for High Tea as dusk was falling.*

*We were further delayed trying to help an Indian party travelling to Pokhara by taxi. Their rear tyre plus two spares had numerous blow outs and punctures. Wanted to borrow our spare but luckily it wouldn't fit. We lent them tyre levers, pump, repair kit and pressure gauge and let them get on with it. Arrived fairly late at Pokhara but at least we knew where we were going and we didn't get bogged. Had a quick beer with Beryl and Dianne did her packing as they were supposed to be leaving early on their trek the next morning.*

**Dianne:** *To bank and then to Aunt Janes for last delicious dinner then onto Pokhara. Himalayas must have known we were leaving as it was clear all the way with majestic mountains towering over Katmandu behind the terraced fields and river. Peaceful tea break then pleasant drive to Pokhara were we saw the mountains in the moonlight. Got to lake about 9pm and met Beryl – plans to join them on the trek, starting tomorrow, confirmed.*

### Day 144 (Wednesday 22nd March) – Farewell to Dianne

**Julian:** *The trekking party didn't get away until 9.30am and that was bye bye to Dianne. Spent the morning working on the car. Changed the oil, oil filter, plugs, air cleaner and knocked out the dent in the door. In afternoon went out to change money and then onto the Tibetan Handicrafts and the town. Tried to buy rice wine without any success. A dull day and overcast. Ate out that evening, or at least it was the most disgusting 'Roast Pork and Chips and Veg' we have ever tasted. We only paid for two and then went to have pancakes and coffee at another place. What a disappointment.*

### Day 145 (Thursday 23rd March) – Relaxing

**Julian:** *Decided to spend a second day at Pokhara. Didn't seem to do much. Washing in the morning, swimming with the kids on the Lilo and a few odd jobs on the car. The day was beautifully clear, and we had gorgeous views of the* *mountains. Becky wrote masses of postcards in the evening.*

## Day 146 (Friday 24th March) – 'Bakshish'

**Julian:** *We seemed to get packed up and off at a reasonable time but a frustrating and slow exit from Pokhara. After shopping, coffee out, finding the Post Office which was still closed and filling up with petrol twice, (decided that the first fill would not get us to the border; luckily accepted Indian Rupees), we eventually left. I then wanted to stop several times for photos which really weren't worthwhile anyhow because it was again cloudy, and the kids all had the squits, which required constant stops.*

*Again, a slow and frustrating drive over rotten roads, anyhow we made the border just before dark and spent about an hour and a half getting through. Camped soon after that in the grounds of a guest house. Masses of 'shitty' washing to do and I got blisters pumping water. That day we had seen numerous painted up to the eyeballs and had come across a friendly crowd who wanted 'Bakshish'* [small sum of money given as a tip, bribe, or charitable donation], *but it should have been a warning for what was to come.*

## Day 147 (Saturday 25th March) – Holi terror

**Julian:** *Easter Saturday. A nerve-wracking day. It started badly when I had to use physical force to get our change back from the proprietor of the guest house. Grabbed him by the collar and threatened to drag him down to the police station. Luckily, he was smaller than I was and paid up. We left and were immediately assailed by crowds throwing paint. If we had known it was going to be like this we certainly would not have travelled. At one point we were forced almost to a stop by a paint cart which was pushed into our path. We forced our way round, scraping it along our side while the crowd shouted in anger.*

*This was supposed to be Holi Day where the throwing of paint was a sign of friendship, but now it was being used as an excuse for going mad and letting out all one's inhibitions. It really was very frightening. Stones and mud were thrown constantly. Before we realised and had put the shield down the windscreen was shattered in four different places. The car was scarred by numerous dents and scratches and really looked a ghastly mess covered with mud and paint. We thought of retreating into a thick wood for the day but wondered what would happen if we were found so we kept going, closing the windows fast as soon as we saw a crowd.*

*One consolation, the roads were almost completely clear of traffic. Practically no-one was stupid enough to be driving and we made good progress on roads which we had never seen so clear. Anyway, we made Lucknow and after the usual hour or so of wandering round we eventually set up camp in the grounds of the YMCA. They were all very friendly and sympathised with us; one boy went around and did most of our shopping. They wanted us to go to church the next morning, being Easter, but we felt we had to get on.*

'Holi' is the Hindu Festival of Colours, Love and Spring. It celebrates the eternal and divine love of the gods Radha and Krishna and signifies the triumph of good over evil. Holi also celebrates the arrival of Spring in India, the end of winter, and the blossoming of love. It lasts for a night and a day, starting on the evening of the Purnima (Full Moon Day) falling in the Hindu calendar month of Phalguna; usually the middle of March. It is a playful cultural event and an excuse to throw coloured water at friends or strangers in jest. As Dad says, it is used by some as an excuse to go crazy; which in hindsight makes our decision to travel on this day equally mad.

### Day 148 (Sunday 26th March) – Fuming

**Julian:** *Easter Day. We pushed on to Agra. Still a bit of mudslinging and stone-throwing. One lot of mud came straight through a side window and splattered everything. I was so mad I skidded to a halt, turned round and chased after a dozen or so boys who headed off into the bushes. Stopped and ran on after them and grabbed a small boy from a ditch. Perhaps I was a bit rough on him. He was crying and pleading for mercy. Pity because it was probably the older boys who had inspired the act.*

*Some cheap kites Becky had bought for the kids proved more of a nuisance than anything else. Unfortunately, and stupidly, I had miscalculated on the petrol and we spent the last three hours crawling along at 35 mph hoping and praying. We bought another 7 litres with our last few pennies and our hearts were in our mouths as we entered Agra hoping we would find the campsite without getting lost. We made it without mishap.*

Chapter Twenty-Two

# Agra to Delhi

*Monday 27th – Sunday 2nd April*

Afterater some much needed R&R in Agra, where Mark and I were reunited with the Highway Inn owner's son, with renewed purpose we swiftly made our way back to Delhi. We bumped into some familiar faces and prepared for the next leg of our journey into Afghanistan. Our van springs gave up the ghost again and we were without the camper for a night whilst it was repaired. In trepidation we headed for the Afghan border.

**Day 149 (Monday 27th March) – My purse**

**Julian:** *Decided to rest a day. A slow tidy up. The boys were delighted to see their friend again. With hearts in our mouths again we set off for the bank and garage and luckily made both. The day was hot and the crowds and staring annoyed us. Changed 100 US dollars. Only 200 left. Even so we were spendthrifts and had dinner out at a Kwality Restaurant. Mark puked his little heart up, then stuffed into cream cakes, and Jamie lost his little purse bought in Kathmandu with 2Rp in it. Did a big shop at a nearby store, cheaper than Delhi and then went off to see the Little Taj. Nice but after the real Taj!! Returned to town and found James's purse at the restaurant, bought some beer and returned to camp. Kids were late to bed as they were playing.*

### Day 150 (Tuesday 28th March) – Back to Delhi

**Julian:** *A slow start. Kids were awful and whinged constantly. An uneventful 3½ hour ride to Delhi with kids sleeping most of the way. First stop GPO. Six hundred awaiting us at the Express according to a telegram and curt registered letter which we had to collect from another GPO.* [From Charles, my mother's father 'Grandad', saying how stupid Mum and Dad were and we should never have embarked on this mad journey in the first place!] *Also, two letters from Mum. Took an hour or so collecting money from American Express and met the old couple who had come over on the Chidhabaram. Had an expensive 'I munch' out in Connaught Circus and then made our way to the campsite.*

*At Little Taj and an old beggar we met there.*

### Day 151 (Wednesday 29th March) – Afghanistan visas

**Julian:** *Campsite was very crowded, and Dr and Mrs Davies were still there having had to wait ages for their car part from England. We went down to*

*Afghanistan Embassy to arrange our visas and then had hamburgers etc out in a snack bar, something cheaper than the day before. In afternoon we fought our way through old Delhi out to the gas place where we waited about an hour. We returned via Old Delhi GPO where we picked up a letter from Sue Buchanan.*

### Day 152 (Thursday 30th March) – Van springs again

**Julian:** *Slow to pack up but we could not pick up the visas till 12. Had a farewell coffee with the Davies and left. Having just left the campsite there was a big clunk. At first nothing obvious but after several more clunks it was fairly obvious the spring under Becky had somehow given way. With heavy hearts and still not certain we made our way to the Afghan embassy to collect our visas. On our way back we called in at British Motors and we arranged to have it looked at the next day. Did some shopping in Connaught Circus, sent a telegram to Charles and the boys had their haircut. Returned pretty depressed to the site and booked in again. Parked in another place and had a late lunch.*

### Day 153 (Friday 31st March) – Waiting for news

**Julian:** *Had to get up early to sort everything out. Difficult to know what we might need for living in the tent alone. Got off with the two older boys about 8.50 and drove straight to British Motors. Went straight on the ramp but nothing much to see without dismantling. Left them with it and we went on. I had my haircut.*

*After we looked around the shops, walked around the park in the middle of the Circus and had lunch at the snack bar. We took a look at all the cinemas around the Circus but none had a suitable English film. Checked back at the garage and then took a Rickshaw back to camp to collect passport and traveller's cheques. Bemo back to town with James and Mark where I cashed 50 pounds at the American Express bank. Moped around and looked in several bookshops. Getting really hot so we took refuge in the posh air-conditioned coffee house.*

*At 4pm went back to the garage. The old front spring was out (not broken) and they were trying to replace it with another second hand one found in the market.*

213

*The left hand one was not yet out. It was near closing time so we returned to camp. Had coffee with the Davies and an evening meal out at the restaurant. Beck had got to know Chris and Rebecca and the kids found new friends with their children. James and Mark slept in their tent that night. Coffee with the Irish couple in their van.*

### Day 154 (Saturday 1st April) – Is it fixed?

**Julian:** *Got ourselves breakfast of sorts from the stuff we had saved and ordered tea from the restaurant. Washed and chatted and late morning left with Peter and Andrew in a Bemo to the market at Connaught Circus. First stop nice cool milkshakes. Looked around the market. Saw some beautiful brass horns and brass lamps which we should have bought but we were worried about money. Beck bought a couple of necklaces. Enquired about silk ties and scarves. Very expensive but bought one for Mum.*

*Then off to the garage to collect car. 718 Rp and we weren't even out of the garage before we heard the first clonk. After a test ride they said the spring on the left wasn't seating properly so back to the garage and up on the jack the van went while we went off to the coffee house. 1½ hours later returned. The van looked a lot lower but no more clonks when driven. I reckon they must have put in the second spare set of springs. The original left hand spring had broken but not the welding. A second break was appearing.*

*Difficult to know whether the welding on the rings had anything to do with the change of stress forces thus causing the fractures. Anyway, Dr Davies and someone else seemed to think it might. Mechanic on the campsite did not have a very good reputation as we were now finding out. Spent the afternoon chatting and sorting out. Got some travel tips from Dr Davies and later on Chris and Rebecca came over for coffee. It was 1am before we retired to bed.*

### Day 154 (Sunday 2nd April) – Leaving Delhi for the second time

**Julian:** *Awoke late and very slow to pack up. Masses of washing to do and we still had a certain amount of sorting. Had coffee and sandwiches with the*

*Davies before leaving. Left Delhi without stopping. Felt rather low and on our own. Incredible after only a few days stop how one gets settled in starting to put down new roots and making new friends. We were also worried whether the springs were going to stand up especially as we were already sitting on the rubber buffers. Tired, especially as Andrew had been vomiting all night. It seemed a long monotonous drive across the Punjab plain and we eventually camped at a rest house in a small town 190 kilometres before Amritsar.*

# PART V
# PAKISTAN TO TURKEY
*(3,891 miles)*

~

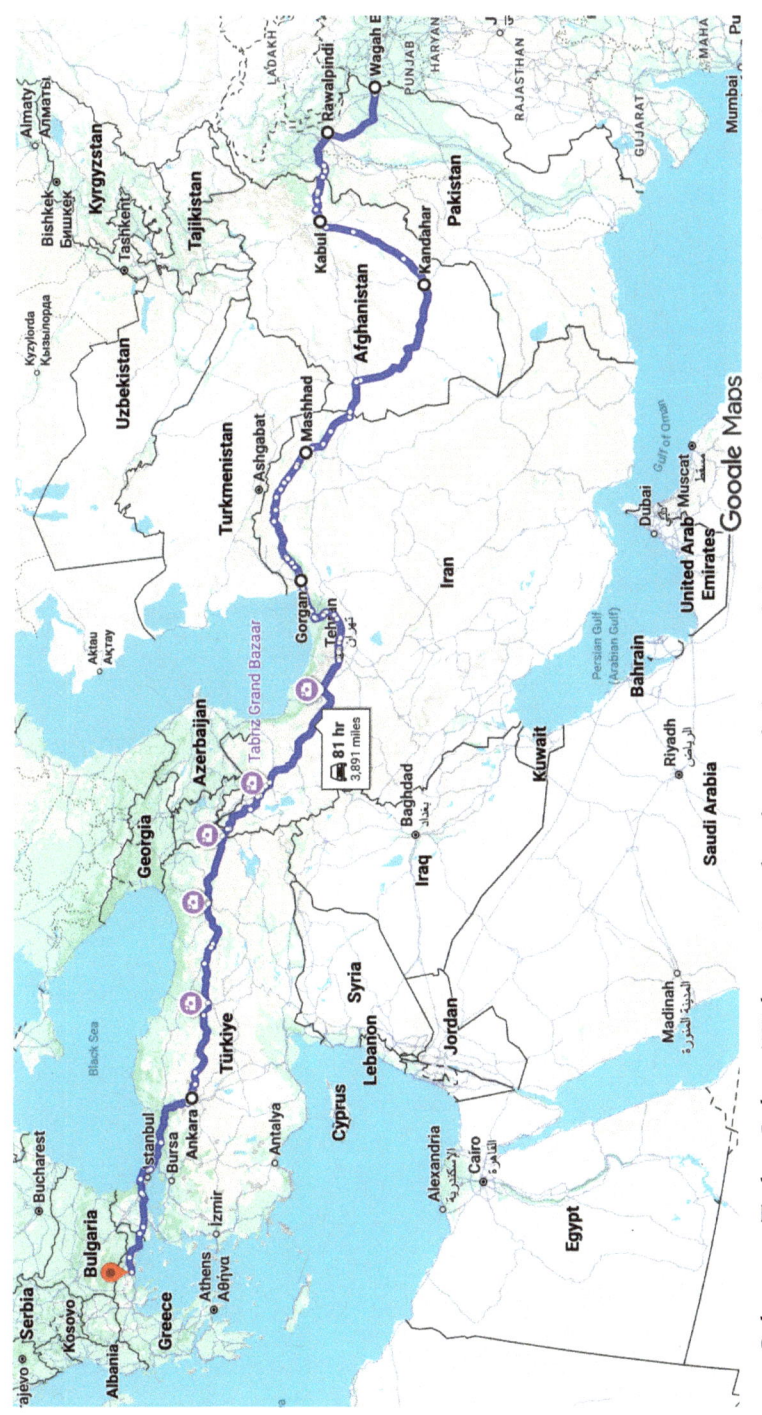

*Pakistan to Turkey: Lahore / Wahga to Rawalpindi to Kabul to Kandahar to Gorgan to Tehran to Istanbul to Kavala in Greece*

Map © 2025 Google

# Chapter Twenty-Three
# Delhi to Kabul
### *Monday 3rd – Sunday 9th April*

After our Nepal adventure, saying goodbye to Dianne and retracing our steps to New Delhi, we embarked on the next stage of our journey, through Pakistan and the Khyber Pass to Kabul, Afghanistan. These were tense times in the region, just before the Russians invaded Afghanistan and Dad gives a sense of this in the diary, but nothing he says will come close to the fear he felt on Holi Day.

### Day 155 (Monday 3rd April) – Amristar

**Julian:** *Pushed on to Amritsar. The usual slow road packed with humanity and animals and we didn't arrive until late lunch time. Called in at the Tourist Bureau but they weren't much help as to where we could camp. Eventually found the Youth Hostel. A relatively modern building with several other overlanders there. Beautiful green lawns and flowers. But the flies were incredible. We had to borrow a fly spray a couple of times. Had a late lunch on the lawn and didn't do anything much the rest of the day. 'Bluebell' the Old GB bus we first saw in Delhi turned up late that night.*

## Day 156 (Tuesday 4th April) – Into Pakistan

**Julian:** *Mad rush to be away early and to beat 'Bluebell' as all the books said the India Pakistan border was bad. One said be prepared to wait up to 8 hours. Only 26 km to the border at Wagah. No real problems. Weren't even searched and we cleared the border in about 1 ½ hours. To begin with, Pakistan looked just like India. The first few villages were filthy with stinking mud, bullock carts, hordes of people. It had, in fact been raining quite hard; we had woken up that morning to some pretty menacing weather. The sky was black and menacing, the wind was blowing and dust obscured everything. Luckily we managed to get the tent down before the rain came. Lahore was a dump.*

*Anyway, things improved. Many more private cars on the road and not so many bicycles, trishaws and Bullock carts. Ford Transit seems to be very popular and Toyota Hiaces quite common. The lorries were much the same as in India but we're very beautifully and elaborately decorated as well as the buses. They were driven at reckless speed but at least they weren't so pig-headed about giving way as were the Indians. We stayed in the grounds of Flashman's hotel in Rawalpindi that night. Rawalpindi was quite impressive after India. It was clean and tidy with trees, shrubs and flowers. Altogether Pakistan was striking us as being a lot more affluent than India. Flashman's was an old colonial style hotel with immaculately dressed servants wandering the grounds and with a swimming pool. No place to pitch the tent so we managed to pack ourselves all into the van it worked reasonably well.*

*Colourful bus in Pakistan and Flashman's Hotel*

## Day 157 (Wednesday 5th April) – Murree side trek

*Julian: We had a lazy morning sunbathing and swimming in the pool. Not bad for 23 RP, just over a pound. Did the usual washing and then after lunch left to do some shopping. The Pakistanis seemed very friendly and very helpful. We decided to do a short side trek and pushed off into the mountains to a place called Murree about 40 miles away and about 7,500 ft up. We actually saw some snow and camped in the grounds of a Lodge House next to a small reservoir. Mighty cold that night. Some beautiful views on the way up. We were at that point very close to the disputed border and Kashmir. The people were very friendly and well wrapped up in cloaks.*

## Day 158 (Thursday 6th April) – Peter's first snow

*Julian: After packing up we drove to a place where we could get to a patch of snow. Peter had never seen snow before and wasn't very impressed with its coldness. I don't blame him. It was rather old and dirty.*

"What's this white stuff?"

"It's cold Mummy!"

*We next went back to town and changed some money. While the formalities were being carried out we all had tea with the Manager. We looked around the shops, obviously a tourist trap with many souvenir shops. It seemed also that many upper class people had their holiday houses up here. Bought two brass lanterns and a cane for Charles. It was getting late so we set off back to Rawalpindi, however not before chatting with the manager of the Pakistan cricket team. Back in Rawlpindi we collected some milk then on to Peshawar, a*

223

*grotty town compared to Rawlpindi, dirty and dusty and crowded. Camped in the grounds of Dean's Hotel. Wanted to charge us 40 RP, which was a bit steep so I complained to the Manager and got away with RP25. Another old-style English colonial hotel with huge deep porcelain baths with unlimited hot water. We really revelled in it.*

## Day 159 (Friday 7th April) – The Khyber Pass

**Julian:** *Away at a reasonable time and not far to the Khyber Pass. Here time seemed to have stood still. Very different from the rest of Pakistan. The landscape was barren with very few trees. The women were all hidden with veils while the men strutted about with their rifles and massive belts full of ammunition dressed up in their full gowns and turbans. They looked very menacing, not the kind of people to get on the wrong side of. It was very dry, the houses and numerous small little forts made of dried out mud. It was what I imagined the Middle East must look like.*

*The Khyber Pass*

*In spite of all the menacing stories about incidents in the Khyber Pass we passed through unscathed. A few people made some menacing movements towards us but nothing could have been as bad as India on that Festival. It was not a formidable pass, no really steep gradient's but it was interesting to see if only because of its history. The mountains looked inhospitable, brown and barren. I'm sure it could get really hot there and camels roamed unhindered.*

*Next step was through the Pakistani customs which didn't take long. The Afghan side was a bit sticky. They wanted to poke their noses into numerous things and had to get the trunk down. We had to enter in the customs declaration forms things like pushchairs and porta potties and playpen. Well we eventually got away and it really felt funny to have to drive on the right.*

*Afghanistan is a beautiful country; we first travelled across a green fertile plane full of colourful wildflowers with snow-capped mountains surrounding us. We stopped for lunch on the side of the road but were shooed away by some aggressive character. Heaven knows why. I'm not sure whether he was army or not. The Afghan people are not friendly. They stand aloof and pay very little attention to the hordes of tourists passing through their country.*

*After lunch we started to climb with fantastic mountain scenery and then into the incredible Kabul gorge. How on earth a road was ever able to be engineered there I don't know. Then out of the Kabul gorge we were on an open plain again with snowy mountains very close to us at 6000 ft. The usual hassle of finding the Friends Hotel but after going backwards and forwards and asking numerous people we eventually made it. Of course, we did not even have a map of Kabul. Several vans we recognised from Delhi.*

*Kabul Gorge*

## Day 160 (Saturday 8th April) – Kabul

**Julian:** *After a lazy arising and wasting time we decided to set out on foot so we could see more of the city but this proved to be a mistake as both Andrew and*

*Peter were grotty and the others were moaning about being tired. After asking several times we made the Post Office where we collected letters from Mum and Kate. The tourist office was more difficult to find. It wasn't where it was supposed to be, so we gave up and had lunch out.*

*Peter promptly weed all over the floor of the restaurant and Andrew would not keep still for a moment. After lunch we found the tourist office and got a long sought after map. We could now get back to camp. On the way however we stopped at numerous shops looking at Afghan coats. They really were very beautiful, but it was impossible to know what would have been a fair price to pay. We bought Peter a little scull cap, Becky a dress and blouse and three beautifully embroidered long-sleeved shirts for the boys. We stocked up on fresh bread and donuts and retired to camp for a high tea.*

## Day 161 (Sunday 9th April) – Sigi's Hell

**Julian:** *We had gathered the previous night that it was practically impossible to get into Iran unless one's cholera jab was pretty recent. Ours obviously wasn't good enough, so in the morning I took the big boys and went off to the tourist office to find out what we could do about it. They directed me to the health centre and said it would be done immediately. We packed up the car and set off. Obviously, this wasn't the place. We were told to go somewhere else. We eventually found this place across the river and incredibly it was done on the spot with no charge. The doctor did not agree to giving Andrew a dose but stamped and signed his card anyway.*

*Back to town where we drove down Chicken St and then to Sigi's Restaurant. Chairs covered in dusty rugs and tables in a courtyard under a half made terrace and a huge chess set in the middle. The pieces were so big and heavy it took an adult to move them. We had a disgusting meal of fillet with potato salad followed by rice pudding. Not up to what we had expected. Paid 300 Afghani and wasted at least half of it.*

*After looking around a couple of shops we went to Azi's Supermarket. By this time Beck was feeling well and truly ill and I was feeling a bit off colour.*

226

*Sigi's or jabs we didn't know. I did a quick whip round the supermarket and then after we went looking for plastic pants. After running all over the city I eventually found two. We returned to camp feeling awful. None of the children felt like eating so we all retired to bed at an early hour. What a night though. I had runs like I had never seen before. Pure water and I must have visited the loo at least six times. Beck did pretty well also. I was thirsty as anything and worrying about electrolyte imbalance. Stuffed myself with Lomotil, Backtrim and Salt and Dextrose tablets.*

Chapter Twenty-Four

# Afghanistan to Iran

*Monday 10th – Sunday 16th April*

This week sounds in many ways like it must have been the toughest week of our trip. Mum was terribly sick and unable to help Dad, who started the week not feeling much better than Mum. With an infamous border crossing from Afghanistan into Iran imminent, perhaps it was just as well that my parents were only capable of putting one foot in front of the other. The lack of photos this week (just one) is also testament to how distracted Dad must have been.

## Day 162 (Monday 10th April) – Sick

**Julian:** *Beck and I were incapable of anything the next morning. Absolutely prostrate. Luckily the kids were fairly good. We eventually arose and dithered backwards and forwards. The van and tent remained a mess throughout the day. We bungled through some washing and I staggered down to the garage with a flat tyre and then to the post office to send some cards. They nearly didn't accept one as it was slightly dirty. By the evening I was feeling slightly improved although Beck was still lousy. Changed a couple of tyres around and put the mended tyre back, Again retired early to bed.*

## Day 163 (Tuesday 11th April) – To Kandahar

**Julian:** *Decided we must push on. I was feeling considerably better though Beck* *was still bad. She could hardly do anything and just wanted to sleep. It was very late before we left the camp site. We went to buy meat and fruit first and then to the bank where we wasted another hour. It was therefore 1pm before leaving town and then we had to fill up with petrol.*

*The road was good and gradually rose to 9,000 ft where we were very close to the snow. It actually was cold during the day and we had to close the windows. We then descended somewhat, the road was good and we could keep up a good average. The scenery was somewhat monotonous, but in some ways majestic. Much of it flat across plains surrounded by mountains in the haze. Still a long way from Kandahar when darkness fell but we pushed on with visions of crashing into unlit toll barriers. The road was generally smooth asphalt but had to be paid for.*

*We eventually arrived in Kandahar about 9.30pm and surprisingly without trouble found the Kandahar Hotel where we all had to camp in the van alone. Much re-sorting and arranging before we retired as the kids were already collapsed. The ants were terrible and we were in a grotty mood.*

### Day 164 (Wednesday 12th April) – Mum still bad

**Julian:** *Beck was really sick and I could do nothing. I felt I was going round the bend with everything that had to be done. The kids were particularly unhelpful. What with the washing and everything we did not get off until about 2pm. We really wondered whether it was worth going on at all. We had intended to stop for a late lunch outside town but the landscape soon turned to scrub and semi-desert. The road was good, Russian built paving stones, mainly flat apart from the small Darugo Pass. Spent the night in the grounds of a hotel in the middle of nowhere, arriving after dark. Of course, there was no water until we made a fuss.*

Dad recalls that on this morning Mum dragged herself to the loo, looked in the mirror and saw her eyes were jaundiced. Strangely enough she was so excited that she definitely was ill (in hindsight presumably Infective Hepatitis) and not just putting it on. He thought he may have told her to "buckle up", having been pretty sick himself but now improved. When she returned to the tent she actually had a big smile on her face that said 'I told you so, I'm ill'!

### Day 165 (Thursday 13th April) – Hepatitis?

**Julian:** *Beck slightly improved but feeling not right yet. Suspecting infective Hepatitis. Stools pale. Got a relatively good start and not far to Herat which we made at lunch time. Decided to book into Heart Hotel which we heard had a swimming pool. Regretted it as it cost 100 AF for a tiny patch of grass, no water in the swimming pool , no hot water and the privilege of being kept waiting a long time. Got frustrated with washing up and clearing up the whole afternoon. Spent hours setting up what should have been a superb stew, which then burnt to a cinder in the bottom of the pressure cooker. Very disappointing.*

### Day 166 (Friday 14th April) – John Maffey

**Julian:** *Packed up and drove to the centre of town. Gathered that border was closed, it being a Friday. This was a blow. Tourist office was also closed, so we couldn't confirm. Also, we were very short of money and banks were closed. After doing essential shopping we looked around for another camping place and eventually found the Narjib Hotel. Very pleased, friendly service, cheap and relatively good food. It was here we first met John and got chatting to him.*

*Had yoghurt and kebabs and peppermint tea and pitched our tent on the grass. Later on we took a walk into town. Didn't buy much and could not find any plastic pants. Took a horse drawn carriage back and found out we had been cheated. Anyway, only gave him 10 Afs as his horse refused to cross over a dug up piece of road. Beck again feeling rotten and went to bed early. Had decided to take John back to Iran. He came over that night and we had a whisky and washed dirty nappies.*

John Maffey was to travel the rest of the way back to the UK with us. Dad, doesn't mention it, but he did spot on some ID, that John was the 'Honorable' John Maffey. I did a bit of digging and found out that he was first in line to become the 3rd Baron of Rugby, being the eldest son of the

231

then Baron, Alan Loader Maffey. His father John Maffey, the 1st Baron Rugby, was Governor-General of the Sudan and a key player in Anglo-Irish relations during World War II. I remember John as kind, lovely man who helped us through some hard times. We became very fond of John, who very sadly had a terminal brain tumour and died in Egypt in 1981. He knew he was going to die and just wanted to travel for the remaining time he had left.

### Day 167 (Saturday 15th April) – The Border

**Julian:** *Well, we set off at a reasonable time with John and it took us about 2 hours to reach the border. No organisation and no-one to tell us what to do. Had been raining ever since leaving Herat, but luckily it was now stopping. One bloke told us to completely unpack the van, another one told us not to bother. Anyway, we eventually got the van over the pit, again no-one helping. The Customs blokes then decided to go off for lunch, but Beck was feeling lousy and turned on the waterworks. It had its effect, the chap said, 'Don't worry Sister', and only gave the van a cursory examination. We were then soon off and after a few kilometres came to the Iran side.*

*Immediately everything seemed more civilised. Modern buildings, men in smart uniforms, but that didn't mean that they were any more efficient. In the middle of passport formalities, they suddenly decided to go off for lunch, so we got our lunch also. Passports were eventually seen to, then a long wait for the Customs. They went through the van thoroughly, every cupboard, wardrobe, roofrack, tried to look under the floorboards, sniffed the tyres, put wires in the petrol tanks, knocked the panels; it just would not have been worth trying to smuggle any Hash through, although Becky suggested a shitty nappy would have been a good place. We had heard some terrible stories about people who had been caught. We got away about 4pm after changing money and getting insurance, about 4 ½ hours all told.*

*Well, we pushed on to Mashhad and had chicken and rice (quite nice) in a roadside café as dusk was falling. Reached Mashhad about 9pm and luckily there were signs directing us to the camp site. And it really was a proper camp site set in quite nice surroundings. Of course, it started to rain again as we were setting up camp. John slept in the tent while we all snuggled up in the van. Clocks at the border had gone forward ½ an hour because of Iranian summer time. Scenery so far had been very monotonous, a really flat plain and straight road, but the black cloud formations streaked with rays of sunlight made things rather interesting.*

### Day 168 (Sunday 16th April) – Gas in Mashhad

**Julian:** *Beck was very poorly again and after arriving late the night before we were slow to get started again. We also had to get gas cylinders filled up. But what a difference from India. It took ten minutes from handing over the cylinder. Anyway it was midday before we left Mashhad. We had hoped to reach Gorgan that day, but it was a slow ride up gradual gradients and against a headwind.*

*Beautiful camping stop by stream between Mashad and Gorgan, Iran*

*We only made about 200 kilometres but as dusk was falling we found a superb place by the side of a fast running stream overlooked by snow-capped mountains. Obviously other people thought so too, there were six other overland vehicles as well.*

## Chapter Twenty-Five
# Tehran to Turkey
*Monday 17th – Sunday 23rd April*

On to Tehran through mountains, several near crashes and a welcome break staying at John Maffey's flat; baths and time for Mum to recover. Lovely people, a trek in the hills, restocking and onward to Turkey.

**Day 169 (Monday 17th April) – Drunken soldier**

**Julian:** *It was quite a beautiful morning and we weren't in too much of a hurry to get away. We made good time that day across open flat plains and then descending a significant way down to the Caspian Plain. This was rather lovely with masses of decidual greenery. The Caspian Plain itself was heavily populated and we never actually saw the Caspian Sea. We were looking forward to a proper campsite which was advertised in our books at Amal but it didn't seem to exist anymore. We camped in a picnic park which was where the campsite was supposed to be. We got pestered by a drunken soldier who said he was 'Police' and then when the real police came along to check and tried to look in the tent I didn't realise and got really annoyed. Anyway, after that we had a good night's sleep.*

**Day 170 (Tuesday 18th April) – To Tehran**

**Julian:** *Well, we continued our way to Tehran over the Pass. Lots of climbing through beautiful mountain scenery following a gorge up through numerous* *tunnels. In one there was a bit of a hold up where a Land Rover had overturned in a smash. Must have been quite high (6,900 ft), Elburz, because we hit the snow line and we stopped to take photographs and throw snowballs. Past the highest mountain in Iran, Damavand, 18,000.*

*The driving was becoming a monstrosity and a joke. The timing of the Iranian in overtaking is non-existent, first come first serve and damn the oncoming traffic. Descending from the pass we soon came to the outskirts of Tehran where the driving was even worse. Several near misses and to get across oncoming traffic one has to take one's life in one's own hands and just push. We stopped for a while at the Air Force Base while John made some inquiries about his pay. Then up towards the mountains to his flat. Bought pizzas for a late lunch and took them back to John's flat. Met Paul whose room we took over. A lazy afternoon relaxing and having baths. Went up to the local shops and bought some baby cereal and plastic pants. Shared in a huge pot of curry that night. Numerous people wandering in and out. Open house. Reminded us of Bronsart Road. Nice relaxing atmosphere.*

Dad's description of life at Bronsart Road London, Hammersmith whilst they were going through their medical training:

"A very open House shared by several Nurses and various Boyfriends. Becky was one of the permanent residents. Pretty well anyone was welcome. I actually had my own flat but spent a lot of time at Bronsart. I remember numerous people would be in and out of Bronsart, some you would know, others complete strangers, but always welcome. If the front door was locked anyone without a key would climb in through the open front window. It was a great place with numerous Parties."

### Day 171 (Wednesday 19th April) – Spaghetti Bolognese

**Julian:** *A lazy awakening with washing of clothes and a day in town. Dropped John off and then fought on through the traffic to the post office. Several letters for us, one from Mum, Kate, Wendy, Anne, Charles. Then back to the supermarket where I found food excessively expensive and had not enough money to buy all that I wanted and Peter had a tantrum. I then had a frustrating drive back to* *the central bank only to get lost and then find it was closed.*

*Kids and I were getting fed up by now so we crept back to the flat through pouring torrential rain with the skylight pouring water in. Bought bread and cakes at the nearby bakery. Walked up to nearby shops later on in afternoon to try and find some dinner only to come back with Kentucky fried for the kids. Need not have bothered as huge Spaghetti Bolognese was manufactured that night.*

*Iran: Pass to Tehran; Andy's first driving lesson; Mt Damavand*

## Day 172 (Thursday 20th April) – A walk in the hills

**Julian:** *John went off on his putt-putt to change Rials into Sterling and I went off to nearby supermarket with Pete, having borrowed 5000 Rials to buy last minute things including tinned meat.*

*Later on that day we had a very pleasant walk up into the hills behind Tehran. James, Mark and Peter came, and John, Alex and Rosemary were our guides. Drove up to the foothills and then started exercising our legs with Pete in the rucksack on my back. Hot at first and quite tiring. Had dinner in a gulley next to a stream and quite impressive waterfall. Lazed around for an hour or two afterwards. Then back down again, unfortunately the chairlift was not working to have fruit drinks at the bottom.*

*A very pleasant day with some lovely scenery. I had all but fallen flat on my face in the stream while helping Mark across. Mark and James were fascinated by a huge tunnel bored right through a building by a runaway lorry. Ate the rest of the Spaghetti Bolognese that evening, most people seem to be going out that evening to films or restaurant. John went out to a film and ended up drunk in a restaurant with Rosemary.*

*Walking in the Tehran hills: rickety footbridge; John Maffey and me; Lunch at the waterfall*

## Day 173 (Friday 21st April) – Tehran farewells

**Julian:** *Did not get away from Tehran until late morning what with repacking the van and saying goodbyes. Had to return once to collect the passports we had forgotten and John had to call in at Alex's flat where he had left £1,000 the night before in his drunken stupor.*

*I was very worried about the brakes which seemed to be pulling excessively to the left. A slow drive to begin with a lot of traffic. Scenery uninteresting, across a flat monotonous plain with mountains a long way in the distance. We camped eventually at rather a nice spot just off a parking place near a river and trees. Becky got her feet wet and muddy trying to do the rinsing.*

*Farewells in Tehran: John Maffey at back; and The Littles and John who travelled back to the UK with us*

## Day 174 (Saturday 22nd April) – Good progress

**Julian:** *An insignificant day of travelling through uninteresting country. Usual pooh and wees! We camped about 40 miles before Maku right off the road in some fields near an irrigation channel. We travelled a good distance that day. The shepherds next morning took an active interest in us.*

## Day 175 (Sunday 23rd April) – Iran-Turkey border

**Julian:** *Filled up to the hilt with petrol at Maku. Lovely views of Mount Ararat to the north. The Iran customs were no difficulty but on the Turkish side it seemed that one got nowhere unless one bakshished. Eventually we took all four kids into the customs office and got immediate attention. Roads immediately got worse in Turkey and the camber was much steeper.*

*Had lunch out at Dogubayazit at a hotel that John had stayed at. Quite a treat.*

*Then on after a lot of debate along the Military Road only to be stopped outside Igda for two hours because of Communist riots (?). Police all over the place. Still a long way to Ezurum up hill and down dale. A long slow climb up a gorge. We were all getting very exhausted as dusk was falling, so we pulled off the road onto a sodden wet patch of grass. Pelted with rain all night long. About 150 km before Ezurum.*

*Mount Ararat*

Chapter Twenty-Six

# Turkey to Greece

*Monday 24th – Sunday 30th April*

As we drove north it became colder and wetter. This week, (the penultimate of our journey), was punctuated by the van getting stuck in the mud, many wonderful people helping us out, blowouts, punctures, and lots of snow. This was very exciting for us boys, who had never seen so much of it; until we realised how much the cold hurt our hands after just a few minutes of snowball throwing! We dropped John in Erzurum to head south to visit a friend and after driving the full width of Turkey, met up with him again in Istanbul where we spent a night before crossing the border into beautiful Greece, reaching Kavala on this evening 45 years ago.

### Day 176 (Monday 24th April) – Stuck!

**Julian:** *Still raining in the morning and we were in a real boggy mess. Packed up with everything including ourselves soaking, and it was really cold rain as well. Of course, the van was bogged completely and try as we might with mats etc we hardly budged. At length Becky flagged down a road maintenance lorry. Really nice men, (who said the Eastern Turks were wild and aggressive). They brought their lorry off the road and immediately got bogged themselves. Well we eventually got the lorry to the top of a rise by piling rocks under the wheels. We then all started on the van.*

*A second and then a third maintenance lorry was flagged down and we*

241

*gathered quite a crew. We piled stones under the wheels and made a track. Eventually, [Becky: Ha Ha Ha, 6 hrs later!], with people pulling with a rope and masses of others pushing from behind, we got the van up the rise. With the lorry going ahead and us all charging behind ready to hook the rope on in case of difficulties we shot down the rise and managed to surmount the verge and onto the road. We all cheered heartily and handed over 200 TL. Beck was … [Becky: 'thoroughly miserable with numb, bare toes and feeling nauseous due to the exertion of pushing car, etc.'].*

*With everything covered in mud we set off for Erzurum, climbing up and up until the rain turned to snow and we were surrounded by white. It was quite chilly although there was no snow on the ground in Erzurum. We stocked up on stores and camped at the back of a BP garage a few miles out west, to try and sort ourselves out. It was pretty muddy there also but we managed to get a few things dried out and caught up a bit on the washing. John went to town to look into coaches south and returned with some goodies only to set out an hour later to catch his coach. It was getting quite cold now, so we retired early to bed in the van.*

*The road to Erzurum*

### Day 177 (Tuesday 25th April) – Proper snow

**Julian & Becky:** *I awake early to find everything thickly coated … in snow including the tent and all our belongings. We couldn't find most of them.*

*The children started off all excited till they realised how cold it was, then they all huddled in the van dripping, making it difficult to pack up. Eventually we got away to a very late start.*

*BP Garage
camp site near
Erzurum*

**Julian:** *The snow quickly disappeared as we descended. A slow drive up and down passing over some magnificent white passes. The road was mainly unmade up and rough, giving the springs a hell of a beating. We had one blowout on that stretch just as dusk was falling. After changing tyres, we made it to the bottom of a hill and camped in the grounds of a ruin which called itself a hotel and paid 50 TL for the privilege of no facilities. Putting up the tent I put the pole through the wall making another place for the rain to come in.*

243

## Day 178 (Wednesday 26th April) – Bye bye carpet

**Julian:** *Well, it was thick frost we had to contend with this morning. Anyway, it soon warmed up and we had a clean out of the van and discarded the carpet, which was filthy and wet with rain, mud and dirt. It was therefore mid-morning before got off. There was another 20 miles of unmade up road. We pushed on trying to avoid the numerous potholes and not making very good progress and eventually camped in the forecourt of a BP garage amidst the oil and dirt.*

## Day 179 (Thursday 27th April) – Sexy magazines and beer

**Julian:** *Nothing much of significance today. A garage man wanted to know whether I had any sexy magazines. Bought some beer in Ankara plus some other stores only to find we had a flat when starting off again. Were lent a hydraulic jack which speeded things up. Had intended to get further than Ankara today but after all this we stopped at the BP MoCamp out west of Ankara. Wasn't yet open so the showers weren't working. Quite a number of other overlanders there camped in the mud.*

## Day 180 (Friday 28th April) – Bridge over the Bosphurus

**Julian:** *We made good progress that day and travelled a good distance until we hit heavy traffic from Izmit onwards where we just crawled. There were several hold ups and having done so well it was so frustrating. We eventually got onto a dual carriageway which we followed to the end and promptly got lost in the smallest side streets possible down by the side of the Bosphorus. Some kind gentleman led us back to the main road in his car and we then made it to the bridge which was quite an engineering feat, just as dusk was falling. Would have been fantastic views if the weather had been clear. We were a long way up but it was overcast and grey and had been raining quite heavily.*

*Another 20km or so along the main west highway before we came to the BP Mocamp. The ground was very wet and immediately got bogged but got pushed out by a horde of Aussies. It was quite dark by now and we were exhausted, and the kids were awful. Really despondent and it was muddy and damp. Just after we crowded into bed a storm blew up with wild winds and pelting, slanting rain. I had to crawl out and cover the skylight, check the windows, and rearrange the tent.*

### Day 181 (Saturday 29th April) – Istanbul

**Julian:** *I took three kids to town whilst Beck did piles of washing. Everything was even muddier than before but at least it had stopped raining. Us lot had a nightmare of a journey in two buses to the centre of town. How more and more people got onto the bus I never will know. Some kind man took pity on us and led us all the way to the post office, showing us where to change buses and even paying our fare on the 2nd bus which was a trolley bus. The kids loved that.*

*Collected pile of mail from the PO including card from John with map of where he was staying. Walked up to his hotel and luckily found him at home. Grotty hotel with bed bugs according to him. This was his third day there. Apparently got down to south of Turkey only to find his friend had moved the day before, and where to, somewhere near Sivas, which was on our route through. So, no tent and he had caught the first bus onwards to Istanbul.*

*Anyway, we went out and had goulash and chips (tiny helpings) and then went to a chemist for inevitable plastics and pins. Whilst he was collecting his belongings from hotel, I took the kids to Topkapi Palace, where we saw beautiful embroidery, thrones, caskets, swords and scabbards all extensively adorned with gold and precious stones. The view from the palace grounds over the Bosphorus was amazing, with the ships on the water, numerous mosques, the bridge in the background and the green foliage and blossom in the foreground.*

*After meeting John again we completed some more shopping including an incredible vegetable market and then caught a train back to a station near the camp site from where we caught a taxi. Things were drying out a bit and Beck had done an incredible load of washing. Quite a repertoire of Rugger songs came from a drunken English crew in the bar that night. Someone's birthday.*
[I wonder what they would have thought if they knew the next in line to

become the Baron of Rugby was in the tent next door!]

### Day 182 (Sunday 29th April) – Into Greece

**Julian:** *Luckily it hadn't rained any more, but the ground was still pretty boggy. However, we managed to extricate ourselves without too much difficulty, only to find we had a slow puncture which had to be changed. The road to begin with was crowded but later on cleared and we made good progress. The scenery was very different now, green with small rolling hills covered in deciduous trees, much more like England. Pulled off on the side of the road for lunch. It was pleasantly warm and the scenery soft and inviting. Laid the wet clothes out to dry.*

*Carried onto the border and got annoyed they wouldn't change all our Turkish Lira. The Duty Free shop there was only interested in foreign currency, not their own Turkish Lira. Both parts of the border were fairly quick. Greek soldiers in beautiful uniform patrolling the bridge. No place to get car insurance as still the May Day holidays. We loved Greece. It looked so beautiful. We carried on late that night and eventually reached Kavala, where we camped on the beach under the fir trees. Other Overlanders there.*

# PART VI
# EUROPE
*(1,796 miles)*

~

*Europe: Kavala to London*

Map © 2025 Google

## Chapter Twenty-Seven

# Greece to Surrey

*Monday 1st – Sunday 7th May*

O ur last week – quite a stretch in 7 days! Mum and Dad had had enough after 6 months on the road. The anticipation of arriving home was building and we were getting excited. But before our return we had to deal with being turned back at the Yugoslav-Austria border, Dad being arrested and finding makeshift tyres for our last 1,796 miles.

### Day 183 (Monday 1st May) – A day in Greece

**Julian:** *As usual we were just about the last to leave. The town of Kavala was really rather picturesque sitting on a precipitous slope dropping into the sea. John had gone for a long walk early in the morning, managing to find one open shop and came back with some breakfast. Halfway through town we realised Andrew's play centre was missing so while John looked for more open shops we returned, or tried to return, to the campsite to look for it. But one-way streets galore and eventually we had to be led back and still had no luck. John found one other shop and I found a third. They showered presents on me such as an extra coloured egg and eventually after all this we were on our way to Yugoslavia with a little food and no money.*

*The scenery was lovely and we kept hitting the coast and as it was a fairly warm day we were eventually tempted to stop for an early lunch, laze and a swim. The Greeks certainly loved their leisure time and thousands were out having picnics*

251

etc. Well we pushed on, refreshed, to Thessalonica and missed the road out, so
we found ourselves on the road to Athens. Fifteen miles out we did a U-turn on
a motorway and got onto a road going in the right direction. This was a good
fast dual carriage way extended with lights all the way to the Yugoslav border.
No red tape at the border and we were soon through.

Managed to cash some money, had coffee and beer and bought some beautiful
pork chops. Still nowhere to get insurance. Onwards towards Skopje and we
camped about 40 miles short in a horrible campsite where the cost was atrocious
(nearly 7 pound,s 240 dinars) and where the wind was blowing a gale. The
water wasn't even warm. Time was two hours back at the border which was a
nice surprise. Some of this may have been in Greece but we never had a chance
to check the time.

## Day 184 (Tuesday 2nd May) – Back in time again

Julian: As we were still used to the old time we made a good start and were
away by 8 o'clock. We at last decided to take the quicker middle road to Belgrade
rather than the coast road which would involve at least an extra day's driving.
We pushed on to Belgrade. The scenery was quite green and not half as barren
as we had been led to believe. We were doing quite well until we met up with
the traffic returning to Belgrade. Must have been the end of the May Day
holidays, the traffic was terrible and we just crawled for mile after mile. There
was nowhere to camp so we just crawled on.

By the time we were nearing Belgrade it was dark, the wind was blowing a gale
and the rain was pelting down. We passed through the suburbs and followed
the signs toward Zagreb and then to our delight we saw a sign pointing to
a campsite. We had to go to a nearby hotel to get money changed and John
enquired the price of single rooms. Not even he was tempted in spite of the
teeming rain. The site proved quite expensive as well, similar to the previous
night but better facilities. We pitched the tent in the sodden earth and John
made it his home again for the night. Luckily the rain was beginning to peter
out a bit.

252

## Day 185 (Wednesday 3rd May) – Death Road

**Julian:** *The shops were once again open and John managed to get a good load of supplies before breakfast. We had driven late the night before but it was nice to be on the other side of Belgrade and on the correct road out. The tent and most other things were sodden but we were getting excited and thinking of being home in terms of four days or so.*

*We pushed on along so-called Death Road every now and then seeing an odd cross and wreath planted on the side of the road. The driving to me did not appear atrocious compared to what we had already experienced. The traffic seemed rather heavy and we again ran into jams before Zagreb. Even though, we did quite well but decided to camp early in a beautiful wood about 40 miles short of Ljubljana. We disturbed some 'Love Birds' and set up camp after nearly getting bogged again. It was though a lovely situation, fairly dry underneath and the kids had a grand time. Managed to air the tent out once again.*

## Day 186 (Thursday 4th May) – Arrest!

**Julian:** *A fateful day. We started off in good time. Hadn't rained during the night and everything was dry. Not far to Ljubljana but we did not recognise it, although we must have passed through it before in the Morris. Funny thought that – at last joined up with 'familiar' territory; Jamie must only have been a few months old.*

*Passed through Jesenice, a horrible industrial town belching coloured smoke. Gradually climbing with snow beginning to appear and beautiful alpine scenery. Buildings certainly had an alpine look, very different from the rest of Yugoslavia. Feeling in a good mood climbed steeply up to the Wurzen Pass and stopped on the side of the road just before the border for lunch. No sooner had we started eating then we were told to 'shoo' by the Military. Too near the border for stopping. The kids had wandered off into the snow and the woods at the side of the road and I'm sure it was pure luck they weren't shot by the patrolling border guards.*

*Well we had to move on quickly up to the border stuffing the rest of our sandwiches into our mouths. One more border to overcome, shouldn't take long we thought. But Oh No, the Austrians wouldn't let us in. The indignity of it! A spot police check. Bald tyres, no go mate. You go back into Yugoslavia and get new tyres. We were bitterly disappointed, fed up and frustrated but there was nothing we could do. So back we went down the southern slope of the Wurzen feeling really depressed. Enquired at several service stations back along the route but obviously they had nothing to offer and directed us back to Jesenice. Enquired at a tourist office where we might find some tyres and were directed to a car accessory shop. 6.50 x 13 Oh No! No such size in Yugoslavia. 175 x 13 nearest thing. The chap kindly came out to the van with a tyre to see if it might fit. Inside diameter fine but outside diameter far too small.*

*Well we decided to seek the advice of a mechanic first and whilst backing the van out I trundled into the wing of a car a stupid Yugoslav had parked and left standing in the entrance of the car park. I was mad especially as the car hadn't been there 2 minutes before. Anyway, he insisted on calling the police who eventually came and demanded to see my green card* [insurance]. *No green card. No one sells them over the May Day holidays. This was getting to be rather a sticky situation. The policemen weren't particularly friendly. We had to follow them down to the police station; he had already confiscated my passport. Trembling I went into the station clutching my papers followed by Becky with the two youngest. She was promptly told to get out. When asked for insurance again I hesitatingly handed over my Carnet. Luckily being an official looking document and the policeman not being able to read English he accepted it as an insurance certificate. When I offered to pay 'Dinars' for the damage the situation was immediately altered. Funny what money can do.*

*I was left alone while the policeman went off with the other driver to test the car. I was terrified what they were going to con me for, so when they returned and wrote down 600 Dinars I wasn't too taken aback. About £20. Certainly would pay that in England for the damage but they probably overcharged me for Yugoslavia. Anyway, we got money changed and paid the 'rotter' off and left the police station hurriedly. I went ahead and bought two new wrong size tyres about 30 pounds each and we left the same car park, carefully this time, in search of a mechanic.*

*Having found one, old innards (far too big) were forced into the new tyres, several punctures were repaired and Russian roulette was played with the wheels. Two innards were beyond repair but luckily I was able to supply two others. We left with one new tyre only half inflated and called in at the service station to re-inflate it and fill up with petrol. We wondered whether to cross the border that night and get it over with and actually changed one more tyre in order to put 'more tread' on the ground in preparation. But we were tired and fed up and there was a camping site just over the road, so with our tail hanging low we set up camp there. John wanted to sleep in the open and as we were now worried about money and wanted to make an early start, we didn't put the tent up. John ended up in a derelict woodshed and it was damned cold that night!*

### Day 187 (Friday 5th May) – 2nd time around

**Julian:** *We set off fairly early and with some trepidation, but at the border they didn't even bother to inspect our new tyres. Changed some Austrian money and again tried to get green card insurance but apparently not required in Austria. Steep descent down the Wurzen to Villach. Remember Dad got stuck halfway up many years ago. Fantastic motorways and we made good time, that is until we had a blow out in one of the new tyres. Nothing punctured, the inner tube must have been pinched. Soon after stopped in a small village where we had the damage repaired. Inner tube was a write off and we had to buy a new one.*

*Picnic in Austria and the Austrian mountains*

*Paid equivalent of £8 for a superb motorway to Salzburg including two fantastic tunnels. Had our picnic surrounded by beautiful mountains on the edge of the motorway. Skirted Salzburg and headed straight onto Munich. Soon hit the next border where we eventually managed to get insurance, damned expensive. Found our way through the suburbs of Munich and headed on west. Eventually found superb camping place in the woods reached by a track from a lay by. Scared we would be seen and told to move on.*

### Day 188 (Saturday 6th May) – Fish and chips again

**Julian:** *A beautiful morning. I took Andy for a walk to humour him while Beck and John packed up. We then pushed on along motorways to Karlsruhe, north to Worm and then West to Saarbrucken and the French border where the customs thought we had been involved in an accident due to the red 'blood' on the van. Soon after we left the motorway and took the N3 to Metz.*

*A quaint little old town with narrow streets. John managed to get money changed while Beck went ecstatic about the shops. I did a bit of food shopping in my best French and then tried to ask our way out of town in my even better French. We eventually found our way onto the smaller roads and headed northwest towards Charleville and Calais. The rain of course started to fall as soon as we entered France. Somewhere near Montmeidy we camped in a Lay-By and again the tent went up in the mud and rain. There was a van there selling fish and chips, which was very welcome.*

**Day 189 (Sunday 7th May) – Home at last!**

The day we arrived back in the UK – no diary entry! My father remembers that we did the Calais-Dover crossing and there was no problem getting a ferry even though we hadn't booked. Dad's final diary entry, written at my request 45 years after the event:

**Julian:** *I do remember standing on deck staring at the White Cliffs of Dover thinking of all we had been through, the Ups and Downs of our Journey and glad we had survived and almost made it. At Dover no real problems but took some time due to Customs wanting to search the van and paperwork involved in importing it. We dropped John off at the railway station and that was the last time we saw of him, although we did keep in touch.* [John very sadly died of his brain tumour in Egypt in 1981.] *I gather he also went down with Hep A. In fact, 71 Park Rd in Chiswick was our first port of call, not Birdshanger* [A house which Mum and Dad jointly bought with close friends Kate and Rob in the early 70's before we moved to Australia], *not Birdshanger. I think we stayed one night, but it was soon obvious that we and Rob and Kate and expanded families were not going to be able to all live there together.*

*Birdshanger – Lala and Grumpy's and our new home in Puttenhanm, Surrey*

*Lala and Grumpy* [our paternal grandparents] *knew we were nearly home but*

257

*didn't know exactly when until we phoned them. We had been so desperate to get back to England that we hadn't really thought about what was going to happen next and where we were going to live, but when we arrived at Birdshanger, Lala insisted that we stayed, although I'm not sure Grumpy was all that keen, especially when I came down with Hep A myself. Eventually, we made that right hand side of the House our own.*

*You probably already know the story about the Infective A. My incubation period had been so long that the GP thought we were now safe and I wouldn't get it. As such and with Becky feeling somewhat better, we started to party and see all our old friends. A bit of a mistake as 26 other people went down with the infection including some of you, although none of you were too badly affected. I was carted off to the Infectious Diseases Ward at The Cambridge Military Hospital in Aldershot* [where Dad ended up working after joining the Royal Army Medical Core in the 1990's].

*Birdshanger, Puttenham: Andy driving again; Andy and big cousin Lolly*

While for Dad Birdshanger really was 'home' – the house where he had grown up – for Mark and I, who had moved to Australia before we could properly remember things, this was a strange place. We too were strangers to the villagers of Puttenham, not altogether welcome at first, given the hepatitis outbreak, I'm sure!

Having made the *Surrey Advertiser* – "Family drives halfway around the world" – two weeks after we returned, Mark and I started at Puttenham

258

First School as two weird and wild, bleach-blond-haired Aussies to our classmates. I was there for less than a term before starting Waverley Abbey middle school in September. I remember that I was paired up with a 'buddy', James Whittaker, who was kind to me and also living in Puttenham, became a good childhood friend. I was totally bemused by the lessons, especially maths, and had to copy my neighbour's work. The excitement of sometimes seeing other camper vans driving past, waving frantically at them, soon gave way to disillusionment when the driver didn't wave back. These were not very friendly people I thought

Very soon however we were embraced by, and embraced, Puttenham as our new home: my mother founding and becoming Chairman of the Puttenham Players local amateur dramatics society; Dad giving numerous talks and slideshows in local village halls about our trip; and Mark, Pete and I quickly, (and a bit sadly I now think), losing our broad Australian accents and becoming true local Puttenham boys. Andy of course, still at less than a year old, had never developed his Aussie drawl. Despite Andy and Pete being too young to remember Mark and I will never forget our experience, and our parents' wanderlust has infected all of us, our wives and our combined ten children – Andy's Brazil and the Welsh Valleys, Pete's West Cork and (currently) hiking the Spanish Pyrenees, Mark's Sofia, Bulgaria and just recently Pretoria, South Africa and myself currently in Singapore.

It's a huge and wonderful world out there – go explore it!

# About James Little

James Little is a father of two boys and lives with his wife and children in Singapore where he runs his own sustainable energy consultancy. He was born in London in 1970, the first son of doctor and nurse, Julian and Becky Little. In 1974, the family moved to Australia, and by 1977 James had three younger brothers. That year, the family's van trip back to England was formative for James and ever since then he has been fascinated by travel – working in the industry for 15 years after studying a master's degree in Tourism Management. *Six Littles go a Long Way* is James' first book – the result of a long-held dream to write up his family's experiences for others to appreciate. It was his 2022 move to Singapore, 45 years after his epic journey, that gave him the motivation to tell the story. This move has also been the inspiration for the planning of a repeat trip in 2027 in the latest sustainably-fuelled camper van – to prove that a zero-carbon motorised journey halfway around the world is possible, and to tell the next story.